Writing Affirmations

**A Collection of Positive Messages
to Inspire Writers**

By Rob Bignell

Atiswinic Press · Ojai, Calif.

WRITING AFFIRMATIONS
A COLLECTION OF POSITIVE MESSAGES TO INSPIRE WRITERS

Copyright Rob Bignell, 2014

Atiswinic Press
Ojai, Calif. 93023
inventingrealityediting.wordpress.com/home

ISBN 978-0-9896723-7-5
LCCN 2014920211

Cover design by Rob Bignell
About the Author photo by Bryan Bignell

Manufactured in the United States of America
First printing November 2014

For Kieran
My favorite future
storyteller...

Contents

Introduction

L ike every kid, I loved a good story. And I consumed a lot of great ones as a young boy, thanks in large part to an illness that kept me inside during recess on cold and rainy days. By myself and with nothing to do, the books in the classroom library became my companions. Together, we dove under the ocean with dolphins and whales, traipsed across the deserts with pioneers and cowboys, and soared into space with astronauts and aliens. My adventures were far more exciting than whatever my classmates were doing outside.

The few days in which I was allowed on the playground were spent play-acting out those tales with my first- and second -grade friends. One of them, whose mother was from Vietnam, lamented after one such visit to the planet Mythra (er, the basketball court) that Mr. Sulu, his favorite "Star Trek" character, never was the hero of the story, whether it be on television, in a book, or during our play.

That served as a revelation of cultural awareness for me. I remedied the oversight that night by penning a one-and-a-half page story, on handwriting practice paper, in which Mr. Sulu saves Captain Kirk's life. The next morning, I gave the story to my friend.

He loved it, couldn't stop talking about it at lunch. That's when another revelation hit me: *I enjoyed writing stories that affected people's lives.*

After that, writing felt natural. My first published freelance article came in fifth grade. I covered wrestling for my hometown newspaper during high school. At college, I wrote and edited the campus newspaper and literary magazine. As an adult, I did the same for both small town and big city papers as well as taught writing to students. Eventually, I started my own professional editing service.

While knocking out a story came easy to me, I've seen many of my reporters, students and clients face a number of self-doubts that hindered their writing. To explain their lack of productivity and craftsmanship, they provided me with an array of excuses: "I'm not much of a writer"; "My idea is no good"; "My writing always has problems in it."

Believe me, I've heard them all.

Over time, I found myself having to inspire them, whether through anecdotes or reasoning, so that they could gain the confidence again to produce the writing that I knew they were capable of – writing that demonstrated their stimulating insights into the world, writing that made me roll in laughter or shed a good number of tears, writing that kept me hanging on every word, writing that compelled me to even change my way of thinking.

Many of them simply needed to believe in themselves and their talents, just needed to have faith in the process of writing. Thus was born this book.

Following is the advice I've given those writers...editing clients who went on to pen bestselling novels, reporters who went on to write award-winning news stories, students who went on to publish collections of poetry.

When reading the advice, stick to just one affirmation per week. Re-read it and the entry that follows three times during that period. Following each reading, do one of the writing prompts appearing after the entry. When the new week begins, move on the next affirmation. If you do, you'll soon find yourself believing in your writing talents and regularly churning out paragraphs and passages that become your short story, novel, poem, nonfiction book or whatever it is that you desire to write. You'll be proud of your work, too, and rightly so.

Every success story begins with a dream. If you dream of being a professional, published author, that success story requires believing in yourself and in knowing that your efforts will lead to triumph.

Now, let's get started pursuing your dream…

WEEK 1

I am a writer.

T hough books you've read may feel magical, the author was no wizard. Rather than wave a wand leading to instant words on a page, the writer worked hard when constructing that short story or book. Most often, that hard work was pleasurable, though, akin to the feeling players of a sports team get when winning. The sweat yielded its own reward.

Authors find pleasure in their work – and so do readers – when living like a writer. No, that doesn't mean having an open booze bottle next to one's notebook or spending days in a coffee shop toiling at a laptop. To be a writer doesn't mean taking on the affectations of famous authors who've come before.

Being a writer means possessing five key qualities or personality traits:

Curiosity

Writers find people, our world, and the self interesting and want to know more. They explore their surroundings and themselves in any number of ways – reading, traveling, experiencing first-hand, and more.

Writers examine their personal beliefs and boundaries and ask questions that others might never even think to raise.

Observant

Writers notice details that define a person or place. They discover behaviors that suggest something more is below the surface and make connections that the average person would not otherwise see.

Love of words
Writers revel in the sounds and meanings of words and sentences and passages; they delight in the poetry of language, feel the fire and ice of words. Anyone can be curious and observant; writers don't express what they've seen or experienced via a painting, song, dance or sculpture, though, but through words on a page. Words are their passion.

Imaginative
Whether writing nonfiction or fiction, prose or poetry, or novels or screenplays, writers are creative. They not only discover intriguing relationships in people's lives and the universe but can weave words about those associations into gripping sentences and passages.

Write all the time
Most important of all, a writer must write. Writers possess not just the courage to share their observations and personal feelings but a fervor for doing so. They feel empty when they do not write, whether it be to inform, to entertain, or to persuade.

>*Spend an hour in a place that you would not normally go to but have always wanted to visit.*

>*Go people watching for an hour at a coffee shop or a sidewalk café. Write notes describing how people converse, how they stand in line, how they order their coffees.*

>*Re-read a poem or children's story that was a favorite of*

yours in childhood. Pay special attention to the wording. Read it aloud to hear the sounds of those words.

WEEK 2

I always am ready to write.

To be a writer, one must write. With all of the modern world's distractions – social media, the demands of work, a house to be cleaned, cell phone texts, a family that needs attention – finding time to write may not always be possible. Even if you set aside a quarter hour every day to write, interruptions may occur.

Given this, you must always be ready to commit pen to paper or fingers to keyboard. You never know when free time will avail itself, and you don't want to miss that opportunity to write. Fostering in yourself the attitude that you are always ready to write is paramount.

How can you do that?

Always keep a story idea in your head

Each morning when you wake up, select a story idea that you will think about through the day. You may be outlining the story, you may be developing images for a specific scene in the story, you may be devising dialogue. Whenever you do mundane tasks – folding laundry, driving to the supermarket, waiting for a meeting to start – use that opportunity to think about your story idea.

Carry a notepad and pen wherever you go

When an idea for your story comes to you, write it down.

Don't limit yourself to that day's story idea; write down any ideas for any story that come to you.

Ask how an object/idea can be utilized in your story

Perhaps you pass a painting in a corridor at work or hear an interesting radio report about the nature of memory. Think about how that painting or insights on memory might be incorporated in your story, perhaps as an image or as a theme.

Sketch during any free moment

Can't think of an idea for your story but stuck waiting in line or listening to a dull speaker in a meeting that doesn't really concern anyway? Use this opportunity to write a description of a person or a location, as if you were an illustrator penciling a rough sketch of a person or a landscape.

>*Keep track of times during the day that you were free to think about a story or to sketch a scene in your notepad. How many minutes did this add up to over an entire day?*

>*List at least a dozen objects you pass each day – the toothbrush in your bathroom, a billboard on the way to work, a tree outside your window. Think of ways these objects might be incorporated into your story as an image or a plot point.*

>*During today's writing session, select any object in the environment where you write – maybe a barista in a coffee shop, a poster in the den, or the refrigerator in the break room. Write a description of this found object, even if it has nothing to do with the story you're working on. The goal is to "train" yourself to write at any moment.*

WEEK 3

Telling myself an idea is no good before I even write it is creativity cancer. I will excise those malignant thoughts!

For many, writing remains merely a hobby. If you find satisfaction in that, that's all right. Many people enjoy sewing but don't make clothes for a living; many people enjoy hiking but don't become wilderness guides. A beloved pastime need not be turned into a career, and a written story or poem never need be published.

Regardless of one's goals, though, virtually all writers want to pen something that they feel proud of. Unfortunately, writers tend to be excruciatingly self-critical of themselves – sometimes to the point that though they yearn to write they can't bring themselves to commit words to paper or computer screen.

You probably are not afraid of writing but afraid of disappointing someone – your readers, your instructors, your family...and most likely yourself. You've become too judgmental of your writing and in doing so feed your fear so it has the power to control you.

Now be honest with yourself: You have no idea how others will receive your writing until you write and share it. Further, writers who are extremely judgmental of their abilities tend to produce quality books because they hold themselves to such a high standard! Your writing actually may be quite well received.

Fortunately, there are many ways you can gather personal courage and dare to write:

Ignore the bullies
Don't listen to your inner voice (or others) who are critical of your writing. Allow yourself to write "poorly" realizing that you'll only get better with each page you pen.

Rethink why you write
Rather than write to master the craft, do so for the journey of self-discovery. Writing then becomes rewarding for reasons other than craftsmanship or being published.

Start small
Rather than attempt too large of a project, such as a novel or even a short story, aim to write a lone paragraph or a single page. Don't set yourself up for failure but work slowly and steadily toward completion of a project.

Write what you're passionate about
Don't write about topics for which you feel no heat. Just because an issue, topic or theme is popular is no reason to waste words on it; write for different reasons than simply being commercially successful.

Never give up
Any goal worth achieving takes hard work. If you want to improve as a writer, if you want to become a respected writer, then you must write.

>*For five minutes, write whatever comes to you, paying no attention to grammar, spelling, punctuation or the quality of the text. Simply write.*

>Select a genre that you usually don't write in. For five min-utes, write a passage in that new genre.

>Join a writers' group, whether it be online or one that meets locally. Share your writing with them.

WEEK 4

There is a voice within imploring me to remember my purpose for being here. Some call this voice their Muse, others call it inspiration. But the voice keeps saying, "Write. Tell your story. Get it on paper." I will listen to this voice and set my course. Until then, I will drift.

If you want to be a published writer, you'll need to write regularly. After all, you can't publish a novel, a short story or a how-to book if you haven't finished it.

That's easier said than done, of course. Most of us must balance our writing time against career, family, friends, house chores and more.

But hours at the office and the needs of children at home need not prevent us from completing our dream book.

So how do you create that "balance"?

First, you must establish a routine, a time every day when

you will write undisturbed, if only for a half-hour. That period should occur at roughly the same time every day. It may mean getting up a half-hour earlier or going to sleep a half-hour later. It may be your half-hour lunch break at work. It may be during the half-hour nap your preschooler takes every afternoon. If your children are older or you're an empty-nester, require others to build their schedules around you for this time. After several weeks of writing a half-hour every day, you'll soon amass quite a number of written pages.

Some authors have told me that if they write for a specified time period, they spend most of their time thinking about what to write rather than actually getting words on a page. If you face the same obstacle and have a little more leeway with your time, instead write to a specific word or page count.

At the risk of sounding contradictory, some authors say if they write to a specific word or page count, they write a lot of junk that later has to be trashed, and so it seems like a waste of time and effort. Don't worry about "wasted" writing, though. Consider that football players don't complain about tackle drills and running plays in practice as "wasted" time since they're not playing a real game – they're simply developing their skills.

Regardless of which approach you choose, don't stop "writing" when your time period is over or once you've reached your word count goal. Keep thinking about your story when jogging, vacuuming, folding laundry, commuting, changing a diaper, waiting for the next meeting to begin, sitting at the doctor's office and so on. Ask yourself what will happen next in the story, imagine a scene, build a character's background. Carry a notepad with you to jot notes or to make outlines.

Once you sit to write again, you'll then have something to work with so you can make your limited time even more productive!

>*List three different times in the day when you will be able to write undisturbed for 15 minutes. Try one time one day, another time the next day, and the third time listed on the following day. Which of those times were you the most creative and productive? Establish that time as your daily writing session.*

>*Carry a notepad with you through the day, writing notes about the story you're working on or other ideas that come into your head. If nothing comes, then determine something specific for your story that you will think about through the day – perhaps a clever image for a scene, a physical reaction of a character, or a line of pithy dialogue. Come up with several potential lines you might write. Use this as the basis to start your next daily writing session.*

>*Chart how many words you write per day. After a week, review it. Does this amount of writing set you on the path of completing your book within a year? If not, can you increase the length of your writing session?*

WEEK 5

Let the powerful energy of your inner muse guide you.

N o one is born being afraid of telling a story. Instead, people learn to distrust themselves. But if they can learn fear, then they also can learn to again trust their creativity and to tell the great tales inside them.

That teachers, editors, family members or even experts have said you never would be a writer doesn't matter. The only voice of any importance is your inner critic.

Struggling with this inner critic is your inner muse who keeps coming up with story ideas, with scenes, with crisp lines of dialogue and intriguing imagery, with outlines of whole books. Writers through the centuries have recognized the power of this muse. The ancient Greeks believed she was a goddess whispering in your ear. The Romantics believed it was the love for a woman inspiring a man. Scientists say it's the way your brain neurons have wired themselves to be creative. Regardless of why it occurs, the fact is that if you enjoy writing and are creative, some inner power drives your passion for penning stories or poems.

If you are to be a successful writer, your inner critic must instead listen to your muse and turn a deaf ear to those who pooh-poohed your writing abilities.

Until that occurs, the inner critic will throw the anchor despite that a good wind pushes your boat's sails of creativity. Don't allow yourself to be stuck in one place.

Embrace your inner muse and let her take you on an incredible journey!

>*Imagine yourself a published, successful writer. Write for 15 minutes as pretending to be that vision of what you one day will be. Did the writing come easier? Reading what you wrote, are you more accepting of your work?*

>*Collect quotations that inspire you to write. Each time your inner critic speaks up, read five of those quotations.*

>*Don't compare your writing to great authors. They spent years developing their skills and talents. Instead, read extremely trashy works by hack authors or in a genre that you dislike. You'll begin to think of your writing as comparatively good and will recognize overused literary devices that you should avoid in your pieces.*

WEEK 6

My mind overflows with great stories. Some rush about like the waves of an ocean. Others meander about like rain through sand. All they need to contain them is a channel of ink and paper.

Ever have an image in your head that would be great for your story, but you just can't think of the right words to use so it gets on paper? You're not alone. Many writers frequently face this problem.

During my years of editing authors' short stories and novels, many have shared with me how they dealt with such struggles. Usually I find out by saying to them, "That was one great descriptive paragraph you wrote! How did you come up with it?" They typically grin, shake their head, and respond, "You know, that was the most difficult paragraph to write! I couldn't get onto paper this jumble of images in my head!"

They then go on to tell me how they worked through it. Generally, it involved one of the following five strategies:

Freewriting

Rather than stress over getting the wording just right, simply write down everything that comes to mind. Sometimes it will be a list of images, other times it will be a long, run-on paragraph, but whichever approach you use, don't worry about typos, punctuation, capitalization, sentence structure, chronological order, or anything else.

Sensual dissecting

Make a list of what's in your head by describing it through each of the senses. What does it look like? What does it sound like? Smell like? Feel like? Taste like?

Spatial examination

List what an image looks like by describing it section by section. For example, a landscape might be related by looking at the foreground, the middle ground, and then the distance. A person's face might be described by looking at its top (eyes), midsection (nose) and bottom (mouth and chin).

Journalistic scrutiny

Standard newspaper ledes answer the questions of who,

what, when, where, why and sometimes how. Do the same with your scene by telling who you're writing about, what that character is doing, the time of day it is, where the character is, and why she's there.

Concrete details

If you have an image in your head of someone experiencing an emotion, list all of the specific physical details that allow you to recognize what emotion the character is expressing. So don't write that a character is "sad" but instead that he is frowning, walking with a drooping head and hands in his pockets, stifling a sniffle, speaking in a soft voice, and so on.

Each of these methods essentially gives you a verbal sketch of your image or scene. Now, like a master painter, you refine it – in your case as a writer through rewriting and editing.

>Pick one object in your story that you would like to write about. Spend 10 minutes writing a sensuous dissection of it.

>Select one landscape, building or other location in a story that you would like to write about. Spend 10 minutes penning a spatial examination of it.

>Choose one scene from a story that you would like to write. Like a journalist, spend 10 minutes describing the who, what, where, when, why, and how of the scene.

WEEK 7

My writing is in my control.

A ll too often, problems in a writer's life negatively affect the ability to write. Never mind that the personal issue requires attention, draining away valuable writing time. The issue itself distracts the mind, so that rather than focusing on a manuscript, the writer finds this turmoil dominating her thoughts.

In short, unable to concentrate, the writer is unable to be creative.

Rather than think of turmoil as an obstacle to writing, though, embrace the opportunities it provides.

Good writers see every situation as an idea for a story. Indeed, as a good reader you've probably noticed there are any number of books out there that deal with the personal issues you face, that examine the very themes of your life.

How you work your way through this turmoil, the solutions you contemplate and either attempt or reject, and the emotions you experience during this difficult time, all make for a great story. You have plot and characters right before you. Now you can add your own perspective to the pool of literature about this topic, and you have theme.

While turmoil may prevent you from writing at the moment, you certainly can take notes and even outline.

And once you start writing, you likely will find it cathartic. Why?

Because you control your story. While you may not be able to control the variables affecting your personal life, that's not so with your tale. You are the god shaping the universe on your computer screen or in your notebook.

You always can say to yourself, "My writing is in my control."

>*Think of a time you've faced personal turmoil in your life. Write a page about the emotions you experienced during that difficult time.*

>*If undergoing a period of personal turmoil, write a page that continues with one of these writing prompts: "I feel..."; "I desire..."; "I need..."*

>*For five minutes, write down the thoughts going through your head. Then read what you wrote. Spend another five minutes writing down your observations about your thoughts.*

WEEK 8

Time spent writing is productive time.

N ovice writers often tell themselves, "I should be doing something else other than writing." Maybe it's folding laundry, maybe it's working on the project for your employers, maybe it's just relaxing.

Such thinking isn't very helpful to your writing. You either go do that other task (and there always are a thousand tasks one could do) or you spend your writing time not thinking about your book but that other thing you instead might be doing.

You never can be a successful writer, though, if you don't

write. And why would you want to defer your dream?

A satisfying life demands that you possess purpose and passion. To be an author is your purpose. Writing is your passion.

Pursuing any passion and achieving any goal requires effort. If your passion is running and your purpose is to complete a marathon, each day you must practice to handle an increasing number of miles. You don't just run a marathon the first time out.

So it is with writing. You don't write the Great American Novel or the next bestselling self-help book in a single draft. Instead, you must learn the craft of writing and revise your works. Each time you write, you incrementally become better and close on the finish line.

Folding the laundry, completing another project at work, or watching television for the next hour doesn't build your writing muscles. It only leaves them flabby.

>*One cause of distractions is having them in your line of sight. Setting aside the laundry is difficult to do when there's a basket full of clothes before you. Find a place that you can write each day where whatever distracts you isn't visible.*

>*Among the biggest distractions are social media and the Internet. When unable to come up with the next line, the urge is strong to answer the latest email or to troll through our friends' posts. During the time you've set aside to write, turn off your cell phone and close all browser windows. By doing so, do you find you're a more productive writer?*

>*You may feel the reason your writing time isn't productive is because you don't have a way to measure it. If so, consider setting a goal each day for writing – word count, percentage*

of a page, number of paragraphs, or some other way of show-ing success.

WEEK 9

Every moment offers a great opportunity to write.

A passionate writer never can be bored. Every location and situation offers an opportunity to write.

Writing is largely an internal, in-your-head activity, after all. It involves your imagination and creativity, which really are nothing more than combining your memories and thoughts in interesting ways to create new ideas or to better understand yourself and the world. No matter where you are, you can create and therefore can write.

Whenever you have a free moment, no matter where you are, there are many writing activities you can engage in. You might outline your next story; if you already have an outline, go more in-depth with a beat-by-beat listing of what will occur in the next scene. You might continue working on your draft. If you have an Internet connection, you might re-search a process or facts that appear in your book.

Combine being present with your creativity, and your abil-ity to write at any given moment will soar. By being present, you engage your setting through taking in its sights, sounds, smells, tastes and how it physically touches you. For ex-ample, if in a coffee shop, you might see a customer standing in line with arms folded, hear her tapping her foot as she waits for the busy barista to take her order, smell her ex-pensive perfume indicating she is not a person accustomed to waiting for someone else, sense the growing heat of her anger as her foot tapping picks up its pace. In this instance, by simply being aware of your surroundings you've observed – and with your creativity – you can write a passage about impatience.

By being present, even if not working on your current book, you can practice writing by penning passages that can be used in another manuscript. Or you night simply do some journaling, in which you describe a scene or a person in that setting, or simply ponder an idea.

>*Practice being present. Anytime you're waiting, write down what you see, hear, smell, taste and sense through touch. Can you organize these details you've observed into a coherent paragraph that describes this setting?*

>*Open a dictionary or a thesaurus to any page and select a random word. Do this four more times, and carry the list of words wherever you go. When you find yourself with down time, write a paragraph about how the surroundings you are in – the conference room, the landscape passing by you on the bus ride, a store while waiting in line – exemplify that word. Better yet, select the words for your list from a story you're penning, focusing on incomplete images or concepts in your manuscript.*

>*Observe other people while in a public location. As you don't have the full context of what they're talking about or doing, make up a situation they are in – planning a heist, fleeing an alien assigned to assassinate them, deciding where they will hide a dead body, and so on. Now wrap their gestures and snatches of conversation into this situation and create a scene or even a whole story.*

WEEK 10

Every word I write only further proves that I am a writer.

All too often as writers, we wait for "inspiration" to strike. Certainly it does flash, and when it does, the story almost always is a great idea. The problem, however, is in seeing that idea through to its completion, which is a story printed in a magazine or a book sitting on a shelf.

To get there, you'll need some good writing habits.

The good news is that there's really only one good writing habit: You must write constantly.

Having a great idea means little if you don't follow through with the writing, after all. But even more importantly, the quality of this writing during the follow-through will be poor if you have not developed the skills and acumen that come with regular writing. Think of it this way: You can't run a marathon without doing lots of small, conditioning runs.

So how do you develop the self-discipline to write?

Write daily

Somehow you must set aside at least a half-hour, but preferably an hour or longer, to do nothing but write. Don't worry about the quality; it will vary from day to day, but ultimately over time it will improve.

Warm up

Many writers start their writing session start by reading or revising the previous day's work, a sort of warm-up, and then picking up from there. This also helps ensure consistency in the story if the focus of your writing is a longer work, such as a novel.

Don't edit

During your writing sessions, save hard-core editing and rewriting (as well as the chore of formatting for self-publication) for later. While you might start by reading the previous day's writing, don't get bogged down rewriting it. Just do some quick proofreading and move on.

You always should use a writing strategy that's best for you, but always remember one thing: You MUST write. New copy must flow onto the paper or computer screen daily.

As science fiction writer Robert Silverberg wrote, "The process of becoming a writer involves discovering how to use the accumulated wisdom of our guild, all those tricks of the storytelling trade that have evolved around the campfire over the past five or ten or fifty thousand years. Others can show what those tricks are. But only you can make a writer out of yourself, by reading, by studying what you have read, and above all by writing."

>*Part of motivating yourself to do anything is to be in the right mindset. Before sitting down to write today, tell yourself the following: "I am writing for my own pleasure. The more I write, the better I will get at it. If my writing today is horrible, that doesn't matter; it soon will get better – but only if I start writing."*

>*Think about another project that you started but didn't finish. Why were you unable to finish? Are those same obstacles the reason(s) you're not writing regularly? During your writing session, jot down some ways that you might avoid or over-*

come these obstacles.

>Should you have an unfinished story or chapter, begin a 15-minute writing session by revising it. After five minutes of that editing, continue writing the story or chapter where you left off.

WEEK 11

Good writers are made, not born.

You've written story after story, but none of them ever seem to measure up to your favorite authors' pieces.

Meanwhile, the few of your stories that you thought were actually decent won't sell. You're starting to wonder if you have the natural-born talent to be a writer.

Before you start being hard on yourself, we should explore the underlying assumption: that some people are born with a natural ability to write.

No one really knows if such a talent is "genetic." There's no doubt, however, that some people spend their formative years garnering and mastering the skills that later will make them good storytellers. So, with a qualitative "yes," there are people with talent.

But they can squander it. Many become journalists, speechwriters or college professors who never pen the Great American Novel despite their love of writing and literature. Others find their family's needs and the daily grind of their jobs leave them too little time to write.

In any case, there are those with "less" talent who work at making themselves writers – and their writing shines brighter than many who are talented. Remember, George Orwell once was viewed as an average kid with no talent; today, he is considered one of the greatest writers of the 20th century.

So how can you "work" at becoming a "good" writer? Three ways:

Read

Read a lot. Read the great works and authors of your genre, such as Asimov, Bradbury and Heinlein if you write science fiction. Read the great works and authors of all time, like Homer, Shakespeare and Hemingway. You can't be a good writer unless you read quality works.

Write

Olympic weightlifters had to train and practice every day for years to achieve their success. Likewise, writers have to train and practice to reach a level of mastery. Write every day, even if you don't believe what you've penned is any good. It will get better over time.

Get feedback

Placing your manuscript in a drawer for no one else to see rarely leads to improvement. Join a writers' critique group (there are many online), attend writing workshops, hire a manuscript editor (full disclosure here: I offer such a service). See how others react to your work and use their advice to improve.

>*Check out a book from the library or purchase one for your ereader. Make sure the book is from the genre you write in. Set aside 15 minutes every day to read it.*

>*Read the last line of the book you checked out or purchased.*

Use it as a writing prompt and spend 15 minutes writing a story in which it is the opening line.

>Have another person read a manuscript that you have been working on for some time. Use their advice to revise the piece.

WEEK 12

A good writer depression doth not maketh.

All too often, novice writers think that to be successful they must don the cloak of a melancholy, moody artist clad in black as penning books during fits of insomnia or alcoholic inspiration. No doubt, some writers are like this, and the fact that some of the most famous were – the existentialists and the beat writers typically wore black while Hemingway drank continuously – has no doubt contributed to the stereotype that writers are restless and unhappy.

Unfortunately, this also has led many budding novelists to believe that they can't be successful – that they are not "ready" to write – unless in a state of "discontent."

If there is a connection at all between temperament and writing "success," it probably is related to the genre one works in. How does being discontented make one a great mystery writer, after all? That temperament may lend itself to writing more literary works and the more philosophical of the science fiction tales, though.

If there is an overarching temperament that is important to all fiction writers, a compassion for life and others arguably is paramount. Should that compassion lead to discontent and anxiety, then the author can write the kind of stuff of that discontented writers like to read. Hopefully that compassion instead leads to a sense of self-improvement and love of craft so that one can master – or even influence – the genre that you write in.

Since you possess the urge to write, you likely also possess this compassion for life and others. Embrace that compassion, and you will find that you always are ready to write.

>Reflect upon writers' lifestyles that you've heard about on television/radio programs or read about in books. Did those writers possess a compassion for life and others? In what ways? How are their compassions similar to yours?

>What sufferings or misfortunes of others most concern you? Spend a few minutes listing them, then focus on one, telling how you first came to learn of it and what worries you the most about it. This list can be a good starting point for themes that you might develop a story around.

>What genre do you most like to write in? What are some of the stereotypes of writers in those genres (For example, science fiction writers are nerdy, wear thick glasses, and take great umbrage at anyone who misstates a scientific fact.)? How do you stack up against those stereotypes? Are there deeper traits or qualities of writers in that genre that they share (such as science fiction writers being inquisitive, willing to explore esoteric ideas, and share a deep interest in science)?

WEEK 13

Everything I write makes me a successful writer, as one cannot be a writer until actually committing pen to paper or keyboard stroke to computer screen.

Most who write find themselves filled with anxiety and self-criticism when they compare their work to those authors who inspired them to write. And then there's always the frustration that comes when the right word (or even no words) won't come.

As Karl Iagnemma, an MIT roboticist who also happens to be an acclaimed fiction writer, once said, "A lot of people, when they think about writers, probably imagine people wasting time in cafés, drinking a lot and smoking too many cigarettes, and working when the inspiration – whatever that is – seizes them. But writing is rigorous. Writing, for me at least, takes a lot of concentrated work and effort. It takes dedication and the willingness to do the work even when that feeling of inspiration isn't there at all."

Writing may be hard work, but the rewards are worth the effort. Fortunately, there are a number of ways you can get motivated to write:

Keep a project "bible"

Create a notebook of reference materials in a 3-ring binder of loose-leaf paper. Often "inspiration" will strike on one of those ideas. At least it gives you a collection of ideas you can go back to when you don't know what to write about.

Keep a daily log
Track how many words you write and challenge yourself to top it the next day.

Keep a journal
Often the kernels of stories later can be found in your journal.

Keep in touch with fellow writers
They can offer encouragement and provide advice when you're stuck.

Start with free-writing
Sometimes when driving about, you see a billboard that gives you an idea for a vacation. The same can occur when writing – sometimes when writing aimlessly you develop an idea that can be turned into a story.

Stop at a good point
If you've had a productive writing session, put down the pen at a point where you already know what you want to write next. You will not be stymied when starting the next day.

Keep plugging along
No matter the quality of your work or how low your sales are, don't stop writing. The biggest mistake those who want to be writers can make is to not write.

A few writers employ rituals to help them get started writing. But most don't as the rites only delay the actual hard work of writing. As Isaac Asimov once said, "Rituals? Ridiculous! My only ritual is to sit close enough to the typewriter so that my fingers touch the keys."

>*Begin keeping a project bible of stories you wish to write. If you already have such a book, select the very first story in it and spend 15 minutes writing it.*

>*Do you keep a journal? If so, identify a kernel of a story idea that appears in it. Spend 15 minutes writing that story.*

>*Take a fiction book off your shelf. Close your eyes, open the book to a random page, and press your finger against the center of that page. Open your eyes and read the sentence. Make that sentence the opening line of a freewrite that lasts for 15 minutes.*

WEEK 14

Each word you write only yields more words that need to be written.

When you set down a road, you're not limited to that highway. There will be intersecting roads – some gravel, some narrow streets, others wide boulevards and multi-lane freeways – that in turn lead to many, many other roads. A few of these roads will be similar to the one you started out on, but most will offer new vistas, taking you either through woods or across suburban sprawl, either past farm fields or into cities of gleaming skyscrapers.

In much the same way, each sentence you write gives you the opportunity to take your book in an entirely new direction. No sentence should leave you wondering, "What will I write now?" but "Which sentence should I write next?"

Once you write a sentence, think of all the different ways it might be followed. Consider the opening lines to this story: *As Jane examined the dead man, there was a giggle.*

The next line might describe the giggle. What did it sound like? Was it nervous and brief? Did it grow louder into a full-blown laugh?

Or maybe it describes Jane's reaction to the giggle. Is she surprised by another person? Is she disgusted because she finds her friend's reaction inappropriate?

Perhaps Jane herself is the one who giggled. Why did she giggle? Was she anxious? Maybe she feels delight that the man is dead and got what was due to him.

Possibly the dead man is the one that giggled. What does Jane do then? Is she frightened? Is she pleased that her experiment to revive the dead man worked? Maybe the man really isn't a corpse at all but a fellow med student pretending to be dead during a class exercise.

Each of these potential paths in turn leads to hundreds of more possibilities for that third sentence and then the fourth. By the time you've written the fifth sentence, you've generated dozens of potential starts for your story...and even new stories to be told.

You must begin, though, by writing one sentence. After all, you can't explore the world about you unless you pull out of your driveway and set off down that first street.

>Open a novel to a random page and read the first complete sentence at the top of it. This will be the opening line of your story. Now ask the 5 W's and 1 H – who, what, when, where,

why, how – to come up with alternate second lines.

>Should you find your story at a dead end, maybe you need to back up and go down another road. Rather than asking what sentence should come next, think of what sentence could be written in its place. Does this lead you to other roads?

>Stories consist of many different bits: dialogue, the main character doing something, that character's thought, another character doing something to the main character, a description of the setting, just to name only a few. Take a story you are stuck on and write a potential next line using each of these five approaches. Does one of them give you a good idea about how to take the story forward?

WEEK 15

The act of creating is beautiful, whether it be the birth of a baby or the unveiling of a gorgeous painting. Writing is an act of creating. Affirm your belief in beauty by writing.

Perhaps what sets us apart from the animal kingdom is that we create art. Yes, chimps and elephants both have made paintings while whales and dolphins make up songs, but no animal on the planet other than humans creates with such frequency and variety – clothing, painting, music, sculpture, architecture, theater, dance, decorative displays, and of course, literature.

The act of creating itself is beautiful if only because so little else expresses our humanity – or our uniqueness as an individual...or imitates and therefore honors our Creator...or brings pleasure to others who experience what we've created...or expands our understanding of the universe and all contained within it.

Writing is creation. Through writing, we can understand what being human means. We can understand our own self. We can express the word of God. We can bring laughter and tears and deep introspection to our readers. We can store and share knowledge so others may lead better lives.

By writing, we partake in something greater than ourselves. Pick up pen and paper or take a seat at your computer today and create something of beauty.

>Re-read a story or a chapter of a book that you've really enjoyed. As reading, think about what made the passage beautiful. Apply those literary devices to your writing.

>Even the great masters had to learn their craft. Pick up a book about the craft of writing from the library or a bookstore. Apply a couple of the techniques described in the book to your writing. Are the new passages you've written more appealing?

>Read through a few of your most recent writings. What purpose do the writings serve? Do they help you better understand yourself? Are they intended to bring pleasure to others? How does this compare to the purpose of your favorite authors' books?

WEEK 16

My ideas are a shapeless mass that my writing molds into beauty.

T he ancient Greeks believed the objects we created rep-
resented an idealized form of that thing. A sculptor
chipped away at a block of marble to find the perfect
representation of a body; the painter filling the blank canvas
sought to create the flawless likeness of a landscape.

When writing, you are like a potter who takes a shapeless
mass of clay and seeks to mold it into a beautiful vase. The
potter visualizes the size, form, shape and decorations upon
the vase. In the same way, a writer envisions the length,
genre, plot and style of his story.

Rather than clay, words are the writer's natural material.
And just as clay from one quarry might be different in its
texture and color from clay found in another region, so each
word you use is different in its meaning and sound.

True craftsmanship for the potter comes in being aware of
what can be done with the clay and then having the knowledge and skills to shape it upon a wheel and properly fire it
in a kiln. A writer also must be aware of what can be done
with the words before him, of how to string them into sentences that best evoke the feeling and captures the message
of the story.

Where the potter pinches the spinning clay or coils it into
a structure, the writer compresses passages to get the most
out of his characters and descriptions or lays out the plot so
it takes the reader on an intriguing journey worth reading.

And just as a potter might find his fingers have left an imperfection and so remolds the wet clay upon the wheel or just as a sculptor might chip away a bit too much in one area and so revisits that portion of the statue to cover the flaw, so a writer must revise and rewrite paragraphs, passages and scenes to ensure the story best reflects an envisioned form of the tale.

If like the potter and the sculptor you keep at it, eventually you will rub out all of the blemishes in your story – and create a thing of beauty that brings joy and meaning to others, as certainly as any vase or statue does.

>*Before putting pen to paper, visualize your story. Imagine how it would read if in its most perfect form. For example, as writing my novel, "Windmill," I visualized each line being read aloud by a specific radio personality; this guided how I threaded words together and fashioned the passages and scenes.*

>*The quickest way to freeze yourself when writing is to expect perfection the first time around. Yet even the greatest paintings have sections that the artist reworked. Likewise, a writer must do the same with a story. When writing, don't worry about being perfect the first time around. Instead, take your time and then revise those sections you're unhappy with.*

>*If blocked while writing the opening of your story, ap-proach the story sideways. Start in the middle or with a scene that is more fully formed in your head. A sculptor, after all, doesn't have to start with the feet or the crown of the head but can begin at any portion of the statue. He then allows the other sections to coalesce and grow clearer in his head. You can do the same with a story.*

WEEK 17

Every word I write is a seed that I may nurture into a small, beautiful poem or a tall, soaring tree.

Each idea you have for a story is like a tiny seed. Not all seeds grow into beautiful plants, and likewise not all story ideas will yield an impressive tale. Still, most seeds are capable of growing, so long as they are properly nurtured.

You plant the seed for your story the moment you commit it to paper or to your computer's memory. But just as you wouldn't sprinkle seeds in the ground and expect the best, so you shouldn't believe that simply writing the story idea will lead to the next line and then the next paragraph, the next scene, and then the full tale.

Seeds need good soil to sprout. The rich dirt that helps your story spring forward are further thoughts in your head about where the tale might go – its characters, their motivations, their conflicts, the plot that plays out these conflicts, the setting upon which this all occurs. The more nutrients in the soil of your thoughts, the greater the likelihood that a story will rise from that initial seed.

Sunlight and water are necessary to keep a plant growing. You can give your story sunlight by opening your notebook or laptop and setting aside the necessary time to work on it. You water your story when you devise dialogue exchanges while standing in line at the supermarket or play out how the plot might turn as you drive your car to work and then apply those thoughts when you next work on the manuscript.

Unfortunately, sunlight and water encourages weeds to grow about your story. These ugly interlopers threaten to choke off your story, depriving it of much-needed nutrition, sunlight and water. Identify and cut those weeds – the life-sucking adverbs, the shade-killing descriptions that don't move the story forward, the crowding passive voice sentences.

Few gardens planted by novices look perfect. But with each successive year, the gardener's knowledge and skills expand, and their flowers, vegetables, shrubs, herbs or trees grow to be like those in the perfect pictures that appear in books or online. Likewise, so long as you nurture and tend to your story, it and the future seeds you plant naturally will bloom into a beautiful creation.

>*Even if you have the seed of a story idea, imagining how it might grow into something greater can be daunting. Asking yourself some key questions about the story idea, however, can help you develop it. For example, if writing fiction, you might ask: What is the story's main conflict or what upsets the order of the world? Who is the main character that must solve this conflict or re-establish order? What internal conflict does the main character possess that prevents her from going forward to resolve this conflict? What compels her to overcome this inner conflict and re-establish order?*

>*The above questions work well for fiction, but what if writing nonfiction? Some key questions you might instead ask include: What is the one piece of information that I want readers to get from my book? What are some subpoints to that one idea? What are some different ways that this information can*

be explained to readers? Why do my readers need to know this information?

>Sometimes the best way to get the brain moving on a story idea is by getting the blood flowing in the rest of your body. If stuck, go for a walk, a jog, or a bicycle ride. As doing so, carry a pen and notebook and jot down thoughts that come to you about the story idea. You'll likely find that the increased oxygen and new environment helps you brainstorm and work through a problem.

WEEK 18

I have all the creativity I need to be the writer I want to be.

Among the most common advice would-be writers receive is "Write what you know." It's up there with "Show don't tell" and "Use active voice" as writing maxims.

At face value, "Write what you know" is bad advice. It seems limiting and can only lead to dull stories. After all, how many of us lead the lives of James Bond or Princess Leia? How many of us ever have been knights, pharaohs or presidents?

But that's taking the maxim too literally. Storytellers really ought to stick to writing what they know...but that doesn't mean their stories can't be about space opera heroes, ultra-smart detectives or cowboys.

What the maxim really means – in part – is to know your subject matter. For example, if you're going to write about a space war, get your science right. If you're going to write about a Revolutionary War hero, get your history right. If you're going to write about garbagemen, get the description of their labor right. All of this information can be obtained by research and in some cases living the life yourself. Observation also can suffice. Get these facts wrong, though, and your story will come off as hackwork.

What the maxim also really means – in part – is to ensure "real life" is an integral element of your story. A real space hero isn't perfect but possesses foibles and inner fears, just as any human does. The Roman soldier out on the frontier likely misses his home and family just as do today's servicemen stationed in Afghanistan. These details about "real life" must be part of the story so that your reader can identify with the characters.

"Real life" can be expressed in a number of ways; emotions, sensory details, habits, and motivations perhaps rank as the most common methods. The student of ancient Athens will be bored listening to his teacher lecture just as today's student often would be. The caveman appreciates the warmth of the sun on his cheek as much as the modern man who deplanes. The future colonist of a far-flung world taps his feet when he's tired of waiting, just as 21st century Earthlings do. Jealousy over a woman can rend the relationship of two brothers in the time of David just as certainly as it would today.

When told to "write what you know" then, teachers and editors really are urging you to add the emotions, motivations, sensory details, habits and more that you know readers will recognize as "real" and to get your basic facts right.

So, what do you know? Go write it into your story.

>Is there a part of your story that involves something you've

never experienced? A stagecoach robbery? A firefight during war? A refugee camp? Read a book about the topic using the research to inform your writing.

>How can you incorporate "real life" into a story scene involving something that you've never experienced? For example, on an interstellar flight, what are the feelings of loneliness or the fear of being lost in the great emptiness that the passengers feel? Can you draw upon similar feelings you've felt during a long road trip across the Great Plains or a desert to make the scene in your story more real?

>Try writing part of a story from the point of view of a character whose gender is the opposite of yours. What difficulties do you encounter in telling the story? Does your character consist of stereotypes of that gender?

WEEK 19

Your first written sentence is the foundation of all of your dreams.

You dream of being a published author. Achieving that dream necessitates, of course, that you first have a novel, a short story, or a nonfiction book that can be published.

For the moment, forget about editing, formatting, choosing a print on demand house, or marketing your book. All of those unknowns and hazy elements do not matter now. To concern yourself with them is like constructing the roof of a tower before erecting the supporting beams to hold it in place. Sure, learning about those topics in advance helps you better visualize what you're getting into. But that research really doesn't move you any closer to being a published author.

No, the first brick in building your dreams is to write that book, short story or freelance article. And a good place to start is with the opening sentence.

When readers look at your book, the first sentence or two sets the tone of what awaits them. You can't hold off until your third or fourth sentence to coax them to come inside your creation. If you do, they'll put down your book.

That first sentence sets the tone for your writing effort as well. From the opening line springs the second sentence and then the third. If the main character is doing something in that opening sentence, the second sentence must flow from it by telling what he does next. Choose one action over another – say running rather than throwing a counterpunch – and you have a completely different story, as certainly as choosing red brick over a glass pane will result in buildings that look entirely different.

Have you written your manuscript's first sentence yet? Do so now. You cannot achieve your dreams until you do.

>*Stuck for a first sentence? Read an online list of the "greatest" opening lines for novels, short stories or nonfiction books. Which ones did you like the most? Emulate their style. For example, if "Call me Ishmael" is your favorite, you might write "My name used to be Jane" or "Most people call me Jack, but I've never figured out why."*

>*Often the opening sentence shows something out-of-whack in the world. This then sets up the story's central problem that the main character needs to resolve. Look around your house*

and think of what would need to change for a situation to be off-kilter. For example, "Each time I picked up the telephone, no one was there" or "She reclined in my pool chaise as if completely at home, but I didn't have a clue as to who she might be." After writing five such opening lines, select one as your book's first sentence.

>Foreshadowing is another tried-and-true way of opening a story and can be very useful if you've already brainstormed or outlined the story's premise and characters. For example, if the book is about how far one has to go to defend themselves and others they love, you might write, "I'd never really thought about how I would kill someone though I'd certainly given plenty of thought to who I might knock off."

WEEK 20

Every word I write is another stroke that takes me to the shore of a completed book.

Any journey you set out on requires time and at least some hard work. No matter how difficult such travels may be, though, the destination is always reachable. Wrong turns may be made along the way or a cliff then a thicket of thorns may stand between the starting point and your goal, but ultimately with some careful thought, a little sweat, and a never-say-quit attitude, you can overcome those setbacks and obstacles.

In many ways, writing a story or a book is much like a journey in which you are out at sea on a rowboat. Your destination – a palm-fringed island or the published novel fresh from the printing press – beckons in the distance. Though making a straight line for that objective seems sound, the endpoint is farther away than it initially appears. So you row a little harder.

Sometimes rough waves and the receding tide push you back and deeper into the waters. As a writer, this may be the equivalent of rewriting a chapter, or restructuring a subplot, or redeveloping a character.

In the rowboat, you must remain persistent, not allow the ocean swells to sink you; as a writer you must not allow the editing of a piece or the thoughts of a beta reader overwhelm you and keep you from believing in your goal.

Instead you must concentrate solely on rowing...on writing...of dipping oar into water...of pressing pen against paper. After a while, you look up and realize that landfall is indeed closer.

And then, suddenly, the oars no longer can go as deep as they did before...and there's only a few paragraphs left to write. You've reached the sand rising to the beach...the final page of your tale.

At last, you can stand triumphant.

>*Often a vision you can literally see is more achievable than one written on paper. Take some time to make a book cover with your title and name as author on it. Post the cover over your desk or in a spot where you can see it each time you look up from writing.*

>*Making yourself accountable to another also is a good way of motivating yourself to achieve a goal. So tell you family you're writing a book. Tell them it will come out next Thanksgiving. Are you feeling a little pressure? Good. Now go impress*

*your family so you can show off copies of your book to them
before everyone sits down to turkey, mashed potatoes and
cranberries.*

*>Establishing milestones is another way to make progress on
your book. For example, if you write an average of 1000
words a day, and a chapter in your book is about 5000 words
long, in five days you should complete a chapter. Add some
leeway – say a couple of days – to cover holidays, personal illnesses and emergencies. Your first milestone, reachable one
week from today, will be the completion of a chapter. Two
weeks from today, you will reach the milestone of completing
the second chapter. If you miss a milestone, you must write for
a longer period of time during the following week to reach it
and to make the next one.*

WEEK 21

*The pleasure of each word I write
is returned to me multiplied.*

Sometimes objects placed together are greater than the
sum of their parts. A molecule of hydrogen and two
molecules of oxygen are wonderful on their own, but
combined they result in water, which opens the possibility
for whole new worlds. The four Beatles each were great
musicians in their own right, but together they created
music that transcended their individual talents and influ-
enced generations of artists to follow.

Likewise, the words on your page as separate entities are
interesting, but combined into sentences then into para-

graphs and scenes, they produce something greater: a short story, a novel, a poem, a nonfiction book.

As a writer, you gain from seeing your work grow, evolve and ultimately reach completion. Just as a reader finds a completed story more satisfying than any single few sentences from it, so you also will find the larger work personally more fulfilling than a paragraph or two from it. This feeling grows in intensity with each word you complete.

Indeed, think of the great pleasure writing a lone, powerful image or a riveting two-line exchange of dialogue brings you. Now think of how much more gratifying that image will be when strung through your story as a motif or when that dialogue is extended to three, four or five lines.

Imagine the delight you will feel as you finish a chapter and the exhilaration you'll experience at completing your manuscript!

>*Remain in the present when writing. All too often writers put off the enjoyment until some goal, such as the completion of their book, is achieved. Instead, take pleasure in the act of creating, sentence by sentence, as you write. With each sentence you complete, congratulate yourself and smile.*

>*Focus on the present by taking note of what you do as writing. Note the feel of the pencil in your hand or hear the taps of the keys as you type. Concentrate on the words you add, as if hearing them spoken aloud. Zone out everything around you.*

>*Lose yourself in the momentum of your writing. Turn off the automatic spell checker and your inner self-critic and allow yourself to simply write. After you've finished writing, you'll*

likely find that your paragraph or scene is better than you initially thought.

WEEK 22

The beginning of every writing session is like setting down a road unknown.

Any time we begin something new – speaking in front of people we've never met, trying out a new electronic device, driving around a city we're visiting for the first time – there's a good chance that we'll feel a little nervous. Our stomach might tighten, our hands could get clammy, we may even break a sweat. When that physical response occurs, our instincts tell us to *avoid* the danger.

As a writer, you've probably experienced such sensations when pulling the chair up to the keyboard or opening your notebook. Queasiness takes over because you're uncertain what to write or if what you plan to say will be good enough. There's a distinct danger of failing.

Indeed, for writers each new book, chapter, paragraph and even sentence is akin to setting down a road unknown. Each time we begin to write mimics turning onto an unknown road heading into the desert. What if we run out of gas out there? What if we get lost? Who knows what other threats await in that vast emptiness?

There's no reward without risk, though. After all, who knows what great scenery lays ahead, what discoveries may be made, what Eden awaits at the western end of that highway? We never will know – we never will finish the sentence, paragraph, chapter or book – if we do not drive onward.

Even if upon reaching our destination nothing lays ahead but more desert, the journey itself was worth it. With that trek and each one that follows, the next road becomes easier to navigate. The experience alone enriches us.

Yes, we can decide to never set down that highway and instead pull off onto the shoulder. Our queasiness and self-doubts then may subside. But what have you given up?

Only your dream.

>*Failure can be a great a teacher. Look back at other works you've written but "failed" to complete. What was the obstacle that prevented you from completing it? The writing felt flat? No action occurred? The character wasn't interesting? Identify the problem, research some tips for overcoming it (for example, use active rather than passive voice to give writing spunk), and then rewrite the piece utilizing the advice you've read.*

>*Risk means being vulnerable. Accepting that as a writer is vital to developing your skills. So go ahead and try writing something you've never done before – a poem if you write prose, a novel if you've only written short stories, fiction if you write just nonfiction. Don't worry about getting it "right." Your goal is to make yourself more comfortable with taking risks as a writer.*

>*Risk often means mistakes will be made. If you knew exactly what to do and simply had to follow the steps to certain success, there would be no risk. Maybe what you're writing is too safe, given your skills and interests. To grow as a writer, try a*

plot or a literary device you've never used before, such as writing a story involving a murder if you've only written romances. Don't worry about botching the story; you couldn't develop as a writer if you didn't try. Besides, what if you discover you have a real knack for writing mysteries?

WEEK 23

Through the act of writing, a writer learns more about himself than he could ever imagine.

For many writers, the greatest yield from their writing is not a royalties check or the adulation of fans at a book reading. Instead, it's self-discovery.

To that end, many writers keep journals. By writing each or every few days about what occurred to them or their thoughts about some past event, they use the empty page as a friend or a counselor, describing and explaining what most bothers them, all the while making new connections to better understand their feelings, experiences and beliefs.

Even fiction writers whose focus is creating entertaining books enjoy the benefits of self-discovery. In a sense, all authors write about their past. A person is the sum of his or her own personal experiences, and bits and pieces of what has occurred to us can't help but wind up in our writings. A character may be a conglomeration of two people we once knew, a setting may be our cousin's house that we visited each summer, a character's name might be drawn from that kid in third grade just because it sounds right.

In many ways, the writing seemingly directs the author.

Indeed, some writers say the characters told their own story. Of course, those characters were only constructs in the author's mind – and those constructs tell a lot about the author.

Why? Because writing allows us to reposition ourselves so we can see what is otherwise in our mental blind spots or those things about oneself and the world that we neither can see nor understand from the spot where we stand. It's really not much different from reading a book – another person, who has a unique perspective from our own, sometimes can get us to turn our gaze to new ideas, concepts and ways of looking at things. Writing is the neck muscle allowing us to see the important stuff in our periphery.

Often as writers, we are surprised by what we learn about ourselves. It runs counter to what we've thought about who we are. But it is closer to the truth.

And for those writers, the virtues of truth and authenticity outweigh their books' value in gold.

>Journaling often best unveils truths about oneself when it answers a thought-provoking question. If you're uncertain what to write about, try these questions to kick start your entry: What have I given up on? When did I last step out of my comfort zone? If I could give a newborn one piece of advice that would stick with him/her forever, what would it be? Note: What you write also might become the kernel for a great book idea!

>Another way to write for self-discovery is using a journal to pen your "autobiography." Think of your life as a journey. What were the waypoints in your life? What obstacles did you encounter? What is the purpose of your journey and what is your destination?

>*Many writers use journaling to deal with trauma and emotional upheaval. One way to do that is to write about what you need to let go of: bad relationships; habits and behaviors that no longer serve you; grudges and hurts that you obsess about. Just listing any of the above and describing why you feel that you need to let go of them can be enlightening and empowering.*

WEEK 24

Each paragraph I write is like the unwrapping of a wonderful gift. Treat yourself with a present today and begin to write.

Most of us can recall a birthday or a holiday when we received the most incredible gift – One that was fun to play with, one that offered up a challenge from which you grew, one that provided relief from the stresses of life.

Maybe it was a board game, perhaps a science kit, possibly a book that inspired you.

In many ways, writing is a gift – except it's not one you give not to another but to *yourself*.

Writing delivers the pleasure of creating, of shaping something artistic. It is like a game, in which you play out and make choices as trying to reach an endpoint. In short, it's fun.

Writing offers mental stimulation. You attempt to master the craft as outlined in guidebooks by mavens of the profession, following their "instructions" to see if you also can build a "working model."

Writing provides good therapy. Examining the stressors in one's life and learning about oneself can help you work out inner demons, which is soothing and calming. It's like reading a beloved book that takes you to a place of comfort and joy.

Writing imparts a sense of accomplishment. Once you've filled a page with sentences or added a thousand words to your computer document, you point to something tangible, something measurable, that you've achieved. Like being the first to reach "Finish," like hearing a radio broadcast from a science kit you've built, like closing that book after spending the afternoon reading it, you feel a surge of self-pride.

Some psychologists say that giving a gift actually yields more pleasure than receiving one. If so, why not enjoy the benefits of being both a giver and a receiver by giving yourself the gift of writing?

>*When giving a gift, knowing what the receiver may need or want can help you decide what to get. As a writer sitting down for a session at the journal or keyboard, ask yourself what are your interests or on your "wish list" for books to pen. Writing about a personal interest or attempting to achieve a personal goal can result in a more productive and fulfilling session.*

>*Collectors always are easy to buy gifts for; you simply obtain an item that expands their collection. When writing, what do you "collect"? Do you prefer to write descriptive paragraphs of settings? Haiku? Space opera action scenes? Expand your personal collection by spending your writing session working on what you most enjoy penning.*

>*One way to come up with a gift idea is to observe what the recipient is missing in his home. What are you missing in your writing? Does your book need a description of a character's physical appearance? An apt simile? An exciting exchange of dialogue? Spend your writing session giving yourself a gift by penning the missing part of your book.*

WEEK 25

Let your writing time put your mind and body in a peaceful place.

When we sit down to write, we psychically enter a sanctuary. This safe haven is our own personal space where we can say whatever is on our mind, where we can talk about what matters most to us, where we can imagine the kind of world that we would like to live.

Going to this safe haven – that is, undertaking the very act of writing – brings serenity.

Writing allows you to sweep out of your mind the clutter of daily worries and troubles. All that matters are the words on the page before you and the universe that your sentences and paragraphs have created. For a brief time at least, anxieties about paying bills, an ill loved one, and the politics of our workplace vanish, and you enjoy calm.

When writing, your creativity is like the soft glow of an inner candle, lighting the page with scenes and chapters. These tales and descriptions bring a peaceful order to the real world.

Writing heals you. Like a soothing salve or a scented candle, your sentences offer tranquility as you explore yourself and the emotional and metaphysical concerns that vex you, all in the safety of a story or a journal.

You leave each writing session physically relaxed and mentally untroubled. Such is the place you deserve to be.

>*To be a writer, you must find a place where you can write with few distractions. That means no new magazines or books in easy reach, no TV, email or Internet to take your focus off the task. It must be a place where others will not carry on a conversation with you. For some, this place is the kitchen table, for others a den, for yet more the coffee shop. Examine your writing space. Is it a peaceful, serene setting where you can be creative? If not, transform it into such a place.*

>*The human body really isn't meant to perform for hours on end some of the tasks that our modern writing and office equipment demand of it. All too often, our necks cramp from looking at computer screens at slanted angles, our eyes burn from staring too long at the fixed distance of a computer monitor, and our fingers turn numb from the strain of our wrists performing repetitive motions. If you've spent all day working in an office under such conditions, the last thing your body wants to do once you're home at night or for the weekend is to keep it up by writing. Take some time to explore ergonomics issues and see if you can modify your writing space so you can get back to working on that book.*

>*Try writing in a new location. Even if your current writing spot is perfect for you, sometimes a change in scenery can ignite your creativity and productivity in surprising ways. If you always write at home in your den, try a session at a coffee house or at a local park's picnic table.*

WEEK 26

When I reach for my pen, nothing is out of reach.

T he very act of writing is a testament that anything is possible.

Writing brings reality to what we cannot now do: the technology to travel to other solar systems; use of magical potions to immediately heal an injured comrade; the ability to cross the Old West or sail aboard a Roman galleon. Whether you pen fiction that creates a story centered on these impossibilities or nonfiction that details the path toward obtaining such dreams, writing transforms a vision in one's head into something tangible.

The fuel for this transformation is one's imagination; the devices that this creativity drives vary from pen and paper to keyboard and computer memory, from paperback to ebook.

When our visions become something tangible that others enjoy as well as learn and grow from, they can ignite within readers the desire to make that dream more than just words on a page. The annals of science fiction are ripe with readers who became engineers, scientists and entrepreneurs that made visions of space travel, new communication devices, and medical cures a reality of our modern times. Political, economic and philosophical tomes have spawned new ways of thinking about our world that whole generations then embraced and pursued.

Are you lonely and seeking love? Write a romance. Do you dream of greater wealth? Write a guidebook to investing.

Want to visit mysterious Incan ruins? Write a travelogue or an action-adventure novel.

For with your pen, you can go anywhere and achieve any wish you desire.

>*List five ways you wish the world were different. During your next few writing sessions, develop some story or nonfic-tion ideas that make these wishes "real."*

>*"Impossible" is merely a state of mind. The only reason something is "impossible" is because we lack the knowledge or experience of how to do it (Remember that a little more than a century ago, human flight was deemed "impossible."). As a writer, you are tasked with explaining why something is possible (How does warp drive work? How were some Jews smuggled out of wartime Nazi Germany?). List five things that are widely considered "impossible" then write about how they could occur.*

>*The Walt Disney Company utilizes "imagineers" to create experiences for park-goers. These experiences are built on fantasy and illusion with just the right amount of real-life to be believable. This is not so different from writing a novel, which must offer readers a verisimilitude of reality, also known as the "fictional dream." Read over a recent passage you wrote. Does it feel "real"? Why or why not? Rewrite the piece so that it avoids those flaws that made it feel "impossible."*

WEEK 27

Others dream of writing a book – I am living that dream!

A lmost everyone has a big dream, a fantasy of sorts in which they live the "perfect" life. Maybe it's sailing the waters on a fishing boat, maybe it's traveling around the globe, maybe it's being an astronaut exploring the realms of space.

For writers, that big dream usually consists of writing a book that is a bestseller, allowing them to quit their day job and write in leisure.

Many writers, however, never get past the first element of that big dream – writing the book. They find themselves bogged down with career or school, discover that family eats up their free time, settle for simply maintaining their home. For them, the dream is something they might get to later, maybe in retirement. Maybe...

If you've started your book or short story or poem, how-ever, you've begun to live your dream. Sure, you haven't reached the epitome of your dream, that day when a pub-lisher hands you a million dollar advance and says, "Write whatever you want!" But that's more of the fantasy element of the dream, anyway.

Suppose that your dream is to own your own business. The fantasy element might be to build it into a Google-sized company that you sell to another for billions. The actual dream, though – the part that matters most – is to be your own boss, to manage your company's fate, to grow some-thing that is a legacy to your family. Those who take the leap and become a entrepreneurs are living their dream.

By writing your book today, you are just like that entrepreneur. You are managing your own literary fate, are creating something so that your children and grandchildren will know you as "the author."

Entrepreneurs who start building their own business put in a lot of hard work and thankless hours just to make their first dollar. A writer who's penning a book is at the same stage.

The fruits of your efforts need not have been plucked for you to live your dream. After all, a man is a farmer as soon as he sows the seed, not when the harvest comes in. A woman is an entrepreneur as soon as she opens her doors for business, not when sales reach a predetermined number. And you are a writer the moment you start writing, not when you've sold your first book.

So keep living your dream – write today!

>*What is your dream? In a few sentences, describe what would most make you happy – that is, what would make you feel whole and content, as a writer.*

>*Once you know your dream, to live it you must get your priorities in order. List at least three activities that don't help you achieve your dream (such as watching movies every night, or posting pictures on Facebook) that you might pull back from. Next, list three activities (specifically "write, write, write") that would help you achieve your goals. Cut from your daily life the activities on your first list and replace them with those on your second list.*

>*When pursuing your dream, focus on doing what you love not what brings in money. Many people who really want to be*

novelists take jobs as journalists and ad writers. That's fine if they enjoy that kind of work but often it simply means deferring their dream. During today's writing session, do not worry if your novel will sell or if it has the keywords that marketing gurus want so it can be easily found on the web. Simply write and know that if you do what you love, the money will follow.

WEEK 28

Writing heals my heart like no pill ever could.

A ll too often in our modern day and age, we attempt to cure every ailment with a pill or capsule. That might be fine for our physical aches and for the most serious of mental illnesses, but it's not so wonderful for the moments when we just feel down or stressed out.

Writers, though, know that for those pains a different kind of tablet than the one you pick up from the pharmacist is best for the soul.

Writing itself is a healing activity.

It allows you to detach. When the problems of the world or the heart threaten to crush you, sometimes you simply must toss off the burden. Writing allows you to let go by entering a new world, one in which the ex's latest nasty words or the boss taking credit for the work you did all disappears. They pale to your main character struggling to solve a murder or to you telling the world about the one thing you feel so passionate about.

It allows you to rebuild your self-esteem. Writing is among your many strengths and talents. Being productive at something you enjoy and are good at is like salve on those deep cuts to your ego. Rather than feel defeated when you were passed over for a promotion at work or when your mother lays into you again about still not being married, get up and hit the punching bags with your creativity.

It allows you to have hope. In the world of your novel, you can entertain readers and ensure right wins in the end; through the pages of your nonfiction book, you can give people the knowledge they need to change their worlds for the better. That ability to help others while furthering your own future in turn will inspire you to greater heights.

So here's the editor's prescription, writer: *1000 words daily until next checkup.*

>*Laughter, arguably, is the best medicine. If feeling blue or overwhelmed, counteract those feelings by writing a comedic passage, perhaps for your book.*

>*Crying, counterintuitively to most people, actually helps one heal, as it removes toxic biochemicals from the body while reducing emotional stress. So consider writing a passage that induces weeping. Just keep a box of tissue next to your keyboard.*

>*Fantasizing also can be cathartic. If the reason you feel grief or sadness is because another has wronged you, make a list of all of the things you'd like to do to get back at them but won't because you don't feel like spending the next few weeks in jail. That list isn't off limits to your story's characters, however!*

WEEK 29

Each time I write,
I reaffirm my soul.

D oes the soul exist? Does the question really matter? Even if there isn't a ghost-like spirit within each of our bodies, we recognize that within all of us there is an inner essence that behaves as if it were a soul, something that is individually me. This sense of "me" is unknowable to others.

All too often in these modern times, though, we lose touch with our soul. We're caught up in the material world that says if something cannot be physically sensed it cannot be real. We're trapped in a mass of humanity in which our individual say and views possess too little weight to make a difference.

Writing, however, allows you to reaffirm your soul, to reaffirm your core being.

When writing, the words flow from the essence of who you truly are. When you edit those words, either in your head or on paper, you conduct a dialogue with your very self. You might decide in that conversation whether those words best express who you really are or if they portray yourself as the way you wish to be seen. If honest with yourself, you will seek the words that express who you are.

When writing, if you are true to yourself, you will feel less constrained. The rest of the world expects you to conform to its various standards – dress this way, speak like this, act this way, think like this – but when writing, the only one you're accountable to is *you*. Your characters can dress, speak, act and think any way you choose. Writing liberates you, allows you to express your individuality.

When writing, if you allow yourself to be free, you will recognize your inner beauty. No matter the shape of your body, the color of your hair, or the scars upon your skin, each of us as writers possess the ability to create. That special talent, regardless of how much it has been honed or shaped, is beautiful. And whatever we create is an expression of our innermost self, meaning your very core shines brilliantly.

To break down barriers that separate you from yourself, to be free, to recognize your own beauty, feels wonderful. It is like being told you are loved, that who you are is worthy, that you are cherished. It is a gift of great kindness that you give to yourself.

>*Does your writing express who you are or does it present an image of what you want others to believe? You likely won't be happy with your writing if it's the latter. List at least three values – that is, three ethical principles – that you hold most dear. Do you see those values portrayed in your writings?*

>*What are your individual intentions? That is, what do you most deeply hope to accomplish in life? To live true to your values? To be at peace with the person you are? To inspire others to find serenity and happiness in their lives? List at least three of your individual intentions. How can you incorporate these intentions into your writing?*

>*In a way, writing is like a waking dream meditation (a "vision quest" in other parlance) in which the very essence of who you are utilizes the symbols of everyday things to discover the answers to life's most challenging questions. Which of the "big questions" of life does your writing address? If none at all,*

would your writing improve if you examined the deep questions that you find important?

WEEK 30

Writing won't be an isolating activity for me.

"Writing is a solitary occupation. Family, friends, and society are the natural enemies of the writer. He must be alone, un-interrupted, and slightly savage if he is to sustain and com-plete an undertaking." – Jessamyn West

Writing lends itself to solitary lifestyle. Writers spend time in their own thoughts, and penning that next scene often is done by oneself rather than as an out loud, collaborative activity. Because of this, many who love to write are introverts by nature. But what happens when writing leads to deep isolation that threatens your health?

Indeed, psychiatric research has shown that writers are more likely to suffer from mental illnesses such as depress-ion and schizophrenia. They also have higher suicide rates than the general population.

That shouldn't be too surprising. As writers set upon achieving their goal of publishing a book, sometimes that writing time diminishes the hours available for their fami-lies, loved ones, friends and colleagues. The result is a forced isolation from the world.

That's when loneliness can set in...and it's in just such vulnerable moments that you begin to question your en-deavor and then yourself: *Does anybody even care of I write this book? Will anybody ever read it once published? If they do, is my writing really good enough to be respected by any-one?* Like water spilled on a table, the negative thoughts soon cover the entire surface of your writing efforts from your passion to your creativity.

Of course, some writers are bothered to no end by constant interruption, by having their solitariness intruded upon when creating. Certainly all authors crave a "time" of one's own to write. The challenge is to not allow such seclusion to become a way of life to your detriment, so heed the warning signs given by your feelings of loneliness and separation.

>Talk with other writers. Writing need not lead to isolation. Writers' groups, beta readers, even editors, can talk with you about writing and will understand all the inner tension you're experiencing. Consider attending a writing workshop or taking a class about your book's topic.

>Write in public places. While not a substitute for quality conversation, being around others and interacting with some of them can help lessen the sense of isolation you might get from writing in your own home. Coffee shops, public librar-ies, and cafes all are great places to write.

>Write a little less. Don't lower your standards but lower your output so you can spend time meeting with your friends or being with your family. After all, you can't be a good writer if you find it a negative experience due to forced iso-lation.

WEEK 31

You are not the writer's block you feel, you are not the talentless disappointment you sometimes believe you are. Neither of those thoughts have anything to do with you. You are the one who notices these thoughts – and when you contemplate what you've observed of them, you become a writer.

F inally, you have time to yourself to write – work is over, the kids are away, all homework is turned in – and you sit down before the laptop with a steaming cup of coffee, all ready to write the next Great American Novel.

But nothing comes.

You take a sip of coffee. The mug warms your hands.

Still nothing comes.

You take a long stretch, crack your knuckles, bring your fingers to the keyboard.

Still nothing.

You've got writer's block.

Unfortunately, the longer you allow writer's block to continue, the less you'll have written – and the harder it will be to overcome. Don't fret, though: Almost every writer suffers from it sometime.

Fortunately, there are a lot of things you can do to create the right environment for you to end your block. Here are some methods used by writers that I've edited:

Outline the story

This allows you to jump ahead in your writing but keeps the story focused. Sometimes a scene in your head isn't what comes next in the unwritten story...but television and motion pictures often are filmed out of sequence and later edited to be a coherent whole; though this is done to save money on changing shooting locations, you essentially are taking the same approach.

Play music that will get you in the mood

Heavy metal or industrial pop works if writing cyberpunk, classical if writing about a moment of triumph, Simon and Garfunkel if your character is in a reflective mood.

Conduct a mock interview with your character

Perhaps your character's background and their motivations need to be further developed for you to continue the story. An interview will help the character evolve.

Share your writing with someone

Make sure this person has the caliber to offer suggestions and feedback that spurs your creativity.

Set your story aside for a few days

In the meantime, until you come back to it, read stories or nonfiction works about your setting or in the genre that you're writing, and see if that sparks your creativity. This doesn't immediately solve your writer's block, but it may help in the long run. Often I find "research" about elements of my story inspires new ideas about what to write.

Be honest about what you're writing

Perhaps the reason you can't think of what to write next is that the story is flawed – the plot is illogical, the main character lacks an internal conflict, it's being told from the wrong point of view. In that case, rewrite, start over, or abandon it. Then get to penning a story that works! After you pour yourself another cup of coffee, of course.

>Create a "playlist" for your characters and story, selecting songs that help you get into your character's frame of mind of the scene's tone. Then play those songs as you write. Do you find that you've started writing again? Selecting the songs forced you to think about your characters' personalities, motivations and goals as well as the story's plot.

>If suffering from writer's block, add something that demands explanation, a technique borrowed from author Raymond Chandler. When Chandler had writer's block, he would introduce a man with a gun, which then forced him to figure out who the man with the gun might be and what he wanted given what already had been written.

>Allow yourself to write "poorly." Most writer's block is caused by fear that you lack talent. This probably occurs because you're unfairly comparing the body of what you've written to your favorite authors. Simply start writing and edit out the junk later.

WEEK 32

Every book I've read appears in my writing.

L ooking for a way to hone your writing skills? Try drawing inspiration from your favorite authors' writing.

To some degree, you're probably already doing this. Our perception of what makes good writing often is based on who we consider to be a good writer. If you idolize Hemingway, you'll probably think good writing means short, almost staccato sentences.

There's certainly value in reading and consciously drawing inspiration from the authors you like. After all, they're probably among the best in their genre, so they must be doing something right (pun intended).

Having said this, you don't want to imitate a loved author's style. Instead, respond to his style, to his content. By copying someone else's style and voice, you deny your own. You physically and mentally aren't that author, so at best you only can create a facsimile of his approach to storytelling. The story will ring false to the reader.

By responding to a favorite author's style and content, however, you acknowledge his influence while remaining true to your own voice. As you present the story from your worldview, you've peeled away a level of artificiality (the using of another writer's voice to tell your story). You then become part of an ongoing commentary of all that ever has been written on that topic.

>Read a short story or chapter of a book by your favorite au-

thor. Make a list of at least five things that you like most about the author's writing. Try to incorporate those techniques or styles into your writing.

>Modeling the stories (or chapters) of a favorite author forces you to think about how a story is structured and the characters developed, making writing of your own stories easier later on. Select a favorite short story or chapter of only 5-10 pages and follow its format sentence-by-sentence as writing your own.

>If you really want to learn the craft of writing from your favorite authors, read their inspirations. You typically can find them through his/her personal website or at Wikipedia. You'll be surprised how their best stories don't copy those inspirations, which instead served as a catalyst for creativity.

WEEK 33

Replace your old books with the books you've always wanted to write.

Your love of writing probably arises from a love of reading. Books and the stories in them – whether it be Dr. Seuss' rhymes, the adventures of teen vampires in a YA novel, or a stunning piece of French literature taught in college – brought you great pleasure and left you dreaming of similar tales to be told.

Indeed, authors write the books they've always wanted to read, as another has so eloquently stated.

Your writing skills, after all, are the sum of all that you've learned from writers you've read and that you've been taught via school and guidebooks. While teachers and writing guides mostly shaped your ability to handle mechanics, such as punctuation and a simile, the fiction you've read molded your sense of how to plot a story, of how to introduce characters, of the dialogue between them, of how to present descriptions, and so on.

In addition, everything you've ever read serves as a template for your storytelling. You use the characters you've journeyed with and the universes you've explored via other books as models for protagonists and settings in your own stories. Or perhaps you synthesize the players and worlds from various books. Usually, all this is done without you even realizing it.

What you've read often is a springboard for your stories. As you contemplate the themes and the characters' decisions in your favorite books, you might extend that discussion through your own stories. Or you might wonder what happens next to the characters in those stories (The juvenilia you wrote probably is just that – a sequel to the stories you loved.).

Imitation is the sincerest form of flattery, the old saying goes. Rather than copy, though, why not continue the examination of a subject that your favorite books began (Actually, that author probably continued the discussion as well!)? Today, begin to replace the old books in your personal library with new books that *you've* written.

>*Who are your favorite characters and what are you favorite settings from books you've read? In what way are the characters and settings in your stories similar to them? For example, if you write science fiction, is your main character like*

Captain James T. Kirk and the interstellar community like the United Federation of Planets?

>Do you sometimes find yourself saying, "This has all been done before" as writing a draft? You're probably right. How can your plot, setting and characters differ from those in the books you've enjoyed the most?

>Consider an ethical decision made by a character in one of your favorite books. What would have had to occur in the book for the character to arrive at the opposite decision? Approaching stories from that perspective can give you ideas for new tales to write.

WEEK 34

There is always, always, always something to write about.

"...everything in life is writable about if you have the outgoing guts to do it, and the imagination to improvise. The worst enemy to creativity is self-doubt." — Sylvia Plath

A common question of writers is "Where do you come up with your book ideas?" There's no simple answer – ideas for stories come to writers in a number of ways. There's no easy step-by-step process for developing good ideas.

One thing is certain though – there is always, always, always something to write about. Everything you see, hear, smell, taste or touch holds some story behind it – how it came to be where it is, why it was made, the comfort it brings, and much more.

The key then is to pump the imagination to get ideas flowing. Many good writers use a variety of "tricks" that ensure their imagination never goes dry.

Observe the world

Many ideas come from noticing peculiar aspects of people's behavior or oddities in how the world works. For example, why is that woman in high heels riding a bicycle past the coffee shop window? There's a story to be told!

Get curious about other people and things

Be curious about people and things as related to the meaning and purpose of the lives, and specifically about changes in their lives caused by their experiences. For example, why does the elderly man at the end of the street always shovel every neighbor's sidewalk on Christmas Eve? A story, even if it's one you imagined, sits behind that kind act.

Explore your world

You can discover the world either by actual adventure or vicariously by reading (and then through a diversity in reading materials, meaning don't limit yourself to only those genres you enjoy).

Create maps of imaginary places

Draw coastlines, mountains, cities, nations or star lanes, then develop a story around them.

Distill conflicts into lists

What are incompatible desires and aims that someone could experience? Then match it to an appropriate "What if?" (a situation that aggravates or accentuates conflict). For example, a man wants to advance in his career yet also wants to spend more time with his family. What if on the same day he received two ultimatums – his wife says to spend more time with the family or she'll divorce while his boss says he must ensure a large, time-consuming project succeeds or he'll be let go?

Remember, there's nothing wrong with letting ideas ripen for months or years if necessary. But never forget that ultimately to be a writer, you must write. Even writing a story around what you consider a "bad idea" is better than never writing at all.

>Fictionalize yourself in a difficult situation that someone else faces. How would you resolve the problem?

>Find conflicts in everyday life. Look at the problems those around you are going through and have your characters deal with and rectify those same issues in their universe.

>Place a person you know in a different setting. For example, relocate an urbanite on a Southern farm or a school janitor in a corner office of a high-tech firm. How does their lifestyle and view on life change? You now have a character and a setting. Next, imagine that a problem occurs, upsetting their routine. You now have a plot.

WEEK 35

A story is like a child – though it arises from us, it is its own being.

I f you've ever been a parent or just an astute observer of your niece or nephew, you've probably been struck by how much a child is like his or her father and mother. At the same time, though they share physical traits, interests and patterns of behavior, the child is unique and his or her person.

Likewise, your story is a creation and reflection of you...yet, it is a creature all its own, too.

The universe and characters of your story arise from deep inside you, as if elements plucked from your unconsciousness. You construct the world in a way that your everyday life hasn't yet needed to, and so the story can surprise, leaving you to wonder, "Did I really write that? Do I really believe it?" Similarly, a child also has a mind of his own, one that shares memories and maybe even genetic inclinations to think in ways that the parent does, yet it's still a mind that is separate and distinct, that is essentially unknowable, much like our own unconscious.

At times, the universe and characters you've created are seemingly alien, as if you had nothing at all to do with it. A fictional universe that is sufficiently developed will begin to operate by its own rules simply to be logically consistent, and you may not know all that may occur in the tale, just that it must obey certain, seemingly unknowable laws. Almost all parents have had some experience in which their child did something entirely inexplicable, something that baffled them. But if you could know all that's going in that child's mind – each of her thoughts, each of her feelings, each of her synaptic connections – it probably would make perfect sense, or at least be explainable.

You'll really feel as if your book has taken control of its destiny when readers respond to it. Each reader is like a classmate, a high school sweetheart, or a coworker that a child meets as entering the broader world, interacting with your "creation" in ways that you might not fully comprehend or even be aware of.

All too often, writers think of their story as a machine that they have total control over, that they can fine-tune and redesign. What if we instead thought of our stories as children who we can guide from birth to maturity? What if rather than attempting to fix every problem we approached writing from the attitude of compassionate detachment, intervening when necessary but allowing the story to naturally unfold?

Would our stories then be less of a cookie cutter of ourselves and instead be more real and human to the reader?

>Sometimes writers sabotage their own stories by ensuring every sentence is grammatically correct, as if they were turning it in to their middle school English teacher. Read through many of the great literary works, though, and you'll find enough grammar and mechanical errors to make a spell check program explode. Are you taking the "life" out of your story by smothering it with your red correction pen? Read a paragraph that you've corrected and then the original. Which sounds better?

>Does your story belong in therapy? Perhaps one portion of it appears to be in conflict with another portion, maybe over

tone or theme. The problem might be that we as authors haven't shaped the story enough during its formative stages to ensure the plot, characters and message can adequately address conflicts, motivations and ideas. Consider allowing more discomfort and unhappy circumstances to appear in your story; this may create the right situations so your story can more adequately present and work through plot conflicts, character motivations, and thematic ideas.

>What are the rules that ensure your story is internally consistent? Among them might be that a character will respond in the same way to the same stimuli each time the latter is encountered. The exception would be if your character grows and develops and hence arrives at a different outlook. Look for inconsistencies in your story's plot, characters and theme and then rewrite the passages to correct them.

WEEK 36

Let your characters write their story. They actually know what you want to say.

Novelist Truman Capote once quipped, "You can't blame a writer for what the characters say.

Sometimes when writing, you'll feel as if your characters are directing and controlling their own fate rather than you being the one who shapes them. All of them seem to tell you what they'll say and do. Sometimes their choices may even startle you!

This occurs because if you've created characters with specific needs and motivations, to be logically consistent they must react and respond in certain ways. They also must act within the constraints of a standard plot structure. The universe they exist in may further limit or allow for various behaviors and decisions.

Of course, you do not live in the universe you've created (though it may be an analog for the one you do live in!). Neither might you have the same motivations and desires as your characters, and certainly your life isn't restricted by a series of complications followed by a climactic scene in which all the world is set right. That your characters make choices you wouldn't shouldn't surprise you. They wouldn't react any more like you than might your own sibling (In fact, sometimes your brother or sister may actually make decisions that are more similar to yours than your characters!).

That this occurs only points to the beauty of creating. Just as a parent delights at a child growing up to become his or her own independent, self-reliant person, so you should take pride in your story when the same happens. It's a sign that you've done well as a parent!

>*Just as well-intentioned but misguided parents can stymie their children's shift to independence and self-reliance, so well-intentioned but misguided writers can stifle their stories' growth and evolution. The latter usually occurs because the author forces the characters to conform to his or her personal beliefs rather than be internally consistent based on the characters' needs and motivations. Review one of your stories that you feel doesn't ring true. Is that what occurred in your piece?*

>*One of the major problems with early drafts of stories is that the characters' motivations haven't yet been fully worked out.*

Can you identify you characters' goals and the reasons they want to attain them? Did your characters' goals change from what was presented in the story's introduction?

>Examine how your characters' motivations are presented as the story unfolds. Do their actions and decisions arise from those needs? If not, readers won't view them as realistic because the characters do what the author wants them to do. Instead, the characters should behave like real people with those actual desires and goals. Because the characters are intrinsically motivated rather than the author's puppets, they will be independent and hence "real."

WEEK 37

Not all of my writing is perfect – neither was every step I took as learning to walk.

Ever hit a moment of frustration when you just can't seem to get a sentence or a passage sound right? The result is a brain freeze. You keep working at the line only to suffer through the penning of seemingly even worse lines or passages.

The problem likely is that you are overly judgmental of your own work. To a degree, that is a good thing, as it means you hold your writing to a high standard, and the result is you then produce above average pieces.

If you produce at all, of course…

Taken to an extreme, perfectionism can lead you to never finishing a book through constant rewriting, procrastination, or not even writing at all.

Fortunately, there are a lot of ways you overcome perfectionistic tendencies when writing:

Focus on improving

Writers typically get better with time, so think of your initial writing efforts as the warm-up or the first quarter in a game; it's those writings when you hit your stride during the two-minute warning or on the winning drive at game's end that will be your best work. In short, acknowledge that not all of your writing will be published, but if you keep at it, some of it will rise to the status of being publishable.

Give yourself permission to write a first draft

Acknowledge that the first time a line is written, it won't be perfect. Sure, sometimes it is, and that talent is what inspired you to write a short story, novel or self-help book in the first place. But a few of the lines that follow may be less than perfect, and that's okay. Simply accept that you later will revise your manuscript.

Recognize that your writing is better than you think

Sometimes you just need to get words and ideas on paper and then walk away from them. When you come back to the writing in a week or a month, you probably will be delightfully surprised at how good it actually was, and you'll likely have a more objective perspective that allows you to quickly resolve problem lines or passages.

Establish artificial deadlines

Philosophically speaking, some believe a piece of art is never finished; indeed, writers, musicians and painters often want to revise their works. There would be no novels, songs or paintings if the creating of a piece didn't just stop and their work wasn't released to the world, though. You don't want to revise forever. You can set a deadline of when you will finish a work...and you probably will be surprised by how much your writing actually impresses others!

>*If a line is vexing you, simply place it in parentheses and continue writing the next sentence. Through the day, you can think about what might be written in the spot you skipped.*

>*Place yourself in a situation where you can see or overhear what needs to be written in a passage. For example, if you're uncertain how to describe the way people react when their favorite team scores, go to a sports bar during a big game. If you need to describe two people talking in hushed whispers to one another, go somewhere where people do that, such as a coffee shop.*

>*Simply write something else in the spot that bothers you. Even if you're not satisfied with what you've just written, don't worry about it. In a week, read the passage. Does what you've written now sound fine or does it still need revising?*

WEEK 38

The amount of writing I have done and my skill as a writer grows every day.

Some days you just don't feel like writing. This doesn't arise from writer's block or being overwhelmed by life's many responsibilities. Instead, you obsess about how much there is left to write and find the amount numbing. You've already written a lot and yet have so far to go.

When your motivation nosedives, your inner critic has taken the controls. It's saying, "You're not a writer. You're wasting your time writing. You're not creative enough to fill those pages. C'mon, let's go eat a bucket of ice cream in front of the television together – you'll feel so much better!"

Push your inner critic out of the cockpit. Yes, writing is a lot of hard work and doesn't always go as planned. But you have a vision, one of yourself as a published writer whose books are loved by readers and snatched up by eager fans. Keep a clear vision of what awaits you, and your motivation levels will rise.

After all, your inner critic is wrong. You are a writer, and you haven't wasted your time. Rather than count the number of pages you have left to go (a glass half-empty type of attitude), think of how much you've written (a glass half-full type of attitude).

You've also grown as a writer. With each passage or chapter you've penned, your talent level rose. Maybe the change was incremental and barely noticeable. But you improved. And as you edit and revise your piece later in the writing process, your talent suddenly will jump, like a jet soaring into the sky.

Accept that reaching your destination never is instantaneous. Each moment spent in flight – and each word committed to the page – always will bring you closer to your goal. Your endpoint, your dream, only becomes impossible to reach when you stop moving toward it.

>Re-read some of the writing you did earlier for this book, maybe for Week 2. Then read some of your current writing, maybe something you did for Weeks 36 or 37. Which passage

is better? In what ways?

>If your current writing feels flat, then expose yourself to some new techniques. This can be done by reading a critically acclaimed novel from outside the genre you write in or by discovering a literary device described in a writing guidebook. Try your hand at the literary devices gleaned from the novel or writing guidebook.

>Sometimes to achieve a goal, we need a plan. That plan typically includes an objective and a process for reaching that goal. During Weeks 39-46, we'll discuss a process you can utilize for writing your book. Before doing that, though, you must have a clear goal, such as "I will publish a novel" or "I will complete my self-help book" or "I will write five short stories this year." What is your goal as a writer?

WEEK 39

I trust the writing process to strengthen my writing.

When writing, you probably follow a process – that is, you go through a series of steps from the proverbial germ of an idea to (hopefully!) its publication. The general steps include:

Brainstorming

This is where you come up with the idea. It is those first hastily written notes about your characters, their conflicts, the setting in which the story will occur.

Outlining

Getting down to work, you develop a scene-by-scene plan for what will occur in the story. It may be a classic outline with Roman numerals, a synopsis of each scene, or notes nicely divided onto little 3x5 cards.

Drafting

Next, the outline is fleshed out into actual written scenes from the start of the story to its end. You may write several drafts of a story.

Revising

This ranges from correcting typos to rewriting whole scenes. With each revision, you create a new draft of the story.

Final form

After several drafts, you will arrive at a "final" version. This typically is the one that is published as a book or in a magazine.

Of course, very few people actually follow these steps in a precise, military drill order. You're probably brainstorming as you're outlining, trying to figure out what is the best climax to your story. You're probably revising as drafting, correcting typos and rewriting poor lines of dialogue penned the day before. You're probably creating a new outline for a scene when revising, as you decide the interaction between the characters just isn't working.

Recognizing these steps and knowing where you are with them as writing can be useful. Why? First, it forces you to think about what you're writing, which typically means a more complex and sophisticated work. Only a novice will sit down at the coffee shop, write for a few hours, and think he's come away with a perfect, ready to publish story (Though sometimes a true genius does this!). Writing typically involves a lot of mental sweat.

The writing process also saves you time. For example, if you outline first, you don't have to start all over when your unplanned first draft turns out to be a structural mess. If you brainstorm first, you won't sit at the coffee shop people watching for hours on end because you can't think of something to write.

Finally, it decreases the chance of rejection. If you write a first draft in final form and send it off to an editor or literary agent, chances are you'll be rejected because your story is flawed in a number of ways that you haven't taken the time to address. If it isn't rejected, you're either darn lucky or a literary genius.

>*What is your writing process? Think back to the stories you've completed and write down the general steps you used. Are those steps similar to the ones described above? Are there steps in the process that you don't follow?*

>*Were you taught a writing process in school? What were its steps? How did you respond to it? If you used it, what were your thoughts about how useful it would be for the rest of your writing?*

>*Use the writing process described above to pen a single 5-6 sentence paragraph. How does the final version of the paragraph compare to other passage for which you didn't use the writing process?*

WEEK 40

The lightning bolt leading to every great story is born in a brainstorm.

I f you're putting your pen to paper or fingers to keyboard for the first time on a story, you really aren't starting it at all. You probably "started" writing the piece some time before – in your head.

That "thinking step" is known in the writing process as brainstorming. It is where you come up with the idea for the story; it is that first mad scribble of notes about your characters, their conflicts, where the setting the story will occur, a catchy title and more.

There is no magical answer for making the muse bless you with inspiration. The ways stories come varies greatly, even for authors in the same genre. Some writers only can create when stress free. Others need to be in a tumultuous environment. Some need to delve into good books, examine great art, and listen to fine music. Others need a blank, almost sterile room so their mind can focus.

Regardless, once inspiration does strike, you're ready to brainstorm. In fact, you'll probably just do it naturally (and usually when there's no pen or paper handy!),

The biggest challenge facing you when brainstorming is to prevent your self-doubts from hindering your creativity. Don't tell yourself a story idea is lousy. It may indeed be lousy, but by allowing yourself to explore the possibilities, you might stumble upon an idea that's pretty darn good. Be curious not critical. Criticism comes later when you start outlining your work (which is the next step in the writing process) and lasts through the revising of it.

In addition to generating your idea, brainstorming can involve collection of information to help you formulate your story idea. If it involves a historical romance set in the beginning of the Roman Empire, you may want to read up on the time of Caesar and Augustus. This likely will spur further ideas about your book, perhaps even whole scenes.

In many ways, the brainstorming portion of the writing process is the most fun. It's a time when you let your mind dream freely and your visions soar, leaving practical questions like, "Who is my reader?" (which could alter the plotting and style of your book) for later.

>*List five stories that you've written or started. Where did the inspiration come for those stories? Can you get lightning to strike twice by finding an analogous way to be inspired? For example, if the ideas for a story came from walking through a geologically intriguing setting such as a desert canyon, walk through a different geologically intriguing setting, such as to a waterfall.*

>*Read an article or chapter of a book that relates to your book. For example, if the story is set in western Kansas, read news stories from that area of the state; if the story involves space travel, read about theories for new engines that would power a spacecraft. As reading, jot down ideas that could be used in your story.*

>*Take the following line, "He had a good head start." Brainstorm (and take notes as doing so) who "he" is, what he's running from, why he's running from it, where he's running, and so on.*

WEEK 41

An outline is to a story what a map is to a road trip.

"If you do enough planning before you start to write, there's no way you can have writer's block. – R. L. Stine

Most published writers agree that inspiration is over-rated. After all, inspiration can generate a story idea, a character, or even a scene, but it rarely generates a whole story.

Once a story idea has sprung from your head, you must grow and nurture it. This typically means outlining it.

Some writers prefer getting words on a page to outlining. That may work for some, but for most of us, it'll result in a disjointed story that's missing key elements. Outlining certainly is imperative for a novel and definitely a good idea for a short story.

An outline forces you to think deeply about your story in advance of writing it. Rather than penning passages that must be tossed because they don't fit well into the final story, you can get that first draft closer to publishable form by working out exactly what you want to write. You can ensure the plot will flow logically from opening line through climax, can sketch out characters so that you know them better, can settle on the best point of view all in advance of writing that first line.

In many ways, the outline is like an instruction book for your story. It helps you feed the story with just the right nutrients and to ensure it receives the correct amount of sunlight. You know what you're aiming for even before you sit down at the keyboard.

As with anything, a writer can misuse the outline by over-relying on it. Just because your outline says to write something doesn't mean you have to, especially if it will result in a weak story. Once you start drafting the story (the next step in the writing process), always remain flexible by considering the possibility that your outline contains flaws. After all, as you continue to think about your story, you may come up with better ideas than when outlining.

A side note: There's no right or wrong way to outline. You can use 3x5 note cards. You can write a complex beat-by-beat or even line-by-line plan. You can draw a flow chart on the living room wall. Do whatever helps you best organize your thoughts.

>*Identify a kernel of a story idea in your journal or project bible. Spend today's writing session outlining that story.*

>*Which outlining method did you use for developing your story idea? Note cards? Beat-by-beat list? Flow chart? Did the method work well for you? Select another kernel of a story idea and try a different method of outlining it. Which of the two methods do you prefer?*

>*Reverse engineer a story by creating an outline of it. How detailed was your outline? How much text did the writer include that wasn't part of your outline?*

WEEK 42

Each draft of a book marks another year in the building of a cathedral.

A fter you've brainstormed some ideas and made an outline of how you might organize those thoughts into a story or nonfiction piece, the next step is to get busy "drafting."

A draft is the placement of your thoughts into complete sentences and paragraphs. This might be done in longhand on paper or typed using a word processing program.

When drafting, your goal is to shape the story or article into the perfect piece that you envision it to be. The first time you try to do this, don't worry too much if the piece rambles or is in some way deficient.

That's because you always will complete a "first draft" of anything you write. With each new draft you write, you'll cross out sections that don't work, rewrite sentences or whole paragraphs, perhaps add entirely new ones, select better words to use, put in missing commas, fix typos, rearrange sections, and probably more. But we'll go into that in a future blog entry that examines revising.

In addition, don't presume that you can simply proofread or edit your first draft and be done. You might get away with that if you're an exceptionally gifted writer (or are writing a simple and formulaic piece, such as a news brief, on deadline). While you probably are at least an above average writer, almost all of us need to go through several drafts before arriving at a final product.

>*Convert the outline you created during Week 41 into a first draft. How much did the "written out" version of the story change from the outline? What was included in the first draft that didn't appear in the outline?*

>*Treat a nursery rhyme such as "Jack and Jill" like an outline of a story. Now write a first draft of the story.*

>*Look back at a piece you've previously written. Read it over, and as doing so, revise it. Don't limit yourself to proofreading corrections but ask what structural and organizational changes should be made to it.*

WEEK 43

You cannot improve as a writer until actually revising something you wrote.

As writers, often we are our own worst critics. We're typically either too ruthless or not critical enough of our own stories and articles! Worse, we sometimes even hate the good parts of our manuscript and love the poorly written sections.

Of course, not everything we write is perfect the first time around. Our writing almost always needs proofreading and some revising. The challenge is to ensure your inner editor rather than your inner critic speaks to you.

Your inner critic differs from your inner editor. Your inner critic says, "This is rubbish, utter crap!" Your inner editor says, "I can write this better than it currently is." Your inner critic says you've never been and never will be a good speller and crumples then tosses the manuscript because it reads flat and vanilla. Your inner editor corrects spelling errors and recognizes then revises passive voice passages.

Your inner editor understands that revising involves patching up and reworking your story, not giving up on it. Such revising may require writing new sections or even just starting over. It's sometimes referred to as "rewriting" or "drafting."

Imagine if a contractor came into a building under construction the day the foundation was poured and declared the structure unfit for habitation. Of course it would be. Construction workers have yet to erect the walls. Electricians have yet to install the wiring. Plumbers have yet to connect pipes.

Each draft you write is like a successive stage in this building project. You outline the plot. You add characters and dialogue. You include a description of the setting. As doing this, you notice that some of the action scenes are a little rough and so bring back in your creativity to finish that job. Then you continue with writing the climax, and so on. As the writer, you are not just the contractor but also each of the construction workers for your book.

How many drafts are required? There's no magic number, though usually the less experienced of a writer you are, the more drafts that will be needed. When you feel there's no way you can make the book any better than it is, you'll know you've reached the final draft.

>Learn about specific structural and style flaws that can ham-

per your writing. Troll through books for suggestions about how to address such problems when revising (One book you may find helpful is my "7 Minutes a Day to Mastering the Craft of Writing".). Ask yourself how you can apply these tips to your writing.

>Three general areas you might revise your manuscript for include: structural issues (plot, characters, point of view, etc.); style issues (get rid of the fluff, use active voice, tighten dialogue, etc.); and language arts class issues (grammar, spelling, punctuation, capitalization). For your manuscript, write three separate drafts, with one focusing on structural issues, another zeroing on style matters, and a third on correcting proofreading errors.

>With each draft you write, have beta readers comment on your manuscript. They need not proofread it but should comment on structure, organization, flow and writing style. If you write fiction, they might focus on plot holes, the motivations of any inconsistencies in character, point of view issues, etc..

WEEK 44

Your best writing teacher is a passage that challenged you.

No medical student becomes a doctor simply by reading a textbook. Neither does one become a great painter simply by gazing at the works of great masters on museum walls. Instead, to become qualified to practice her profession, the doctor makes rounds as a resident while the painter actually works with oils and canvas then shows at a gallery.

Likewise, no writer ever became successful simply by reading about a literary device in a writing guidebook. This is not to say that such books aren't useful. They are. Many such books inspire students to read great literature and introduce a number of writing methods to would-be authors.

A far better teacher is actually writing. When that occurs, the writer suddenly becomes aware of the importance of diction, seeks ways to achieve a certain tone, and experiments with differing styles all to achieve a desired effect.

Just as anyone can teach a student the basics, a truly great teacher encourages her pupils to excel, to strive for more than the mediocre. Good teachers challenge their students... and their students rise to the call. A difficult to write passage is akin to that good teacher. Such a passage forces a writer to explore new ways of stringing together words, of experimenting with new plot devices, of examining how other writers did it and then modeling their success.

If you really want to grow as a writer, don't opt for the easy solution by using cliché devices and repeating plots, character archetypes, and unimaginative themes already done ad nauseam in hack books and on television. Instead, accept the challenge of finding a way to take your writing beyond the norm, even if that means going through several revisions.

The result will be a writer who actually can practice his craft with great skill rather than remaining a wannabe who reads about how others do it.

>*When reading how another author might handle a challenging passage, we're really learning from that person's exper-*

ience. That's always a good starting point to determine how you might solve your problem. To that end, identify a passage you're having trouble with in your writing. Now pick up a short story or chapter from a book similar to yours, reading specifically for techniques that writer used to deal with the same kind of passage now posing problems for you.

>Think of a passage you once struggled to write but ultimately completed. How did you work through the difficulties? Can those same strategies be used the next time you face a difficult to write passage?

>Experience alone doesn't make a great teacher. A good learner also observes how he's handling the experience, processes it afterward, and incorporates lessons from it into his life. Given this, think about your writing session from yesterday. What writing difficulties did you face during it (Maybe it was coming up with a plot twist or writing pithy dialogue.)? How did you handle them? What did you learn from the way you handled those difficulties? How might you address those difficulties differently the next time you write?

WEEK 45

I refuse to give up on my writing because I haven't explored every possible way to revise it.

Since writers are close to their work – the universe for the story that is in a writer's head always is larger than the universe for the story that is on paper – they often may not recognize that a passage needs to be revised. Because of this, a troubled paragraph or chapter may go unrecognized by the writer...and if it is recognized, the writer may have no idea how to revise it.

Don't give up on a passage and decide to let it stand simply because you're unclear how to help it work better, though. That simply cheats your reader and your story. You wouldn't give up on your child simply because you're uncertain how to help her, after all, so why treat your story with any less dignity?

If you're thinking of quitting on a passage – or even giving up on the entire writing project – you're simply responding with emotion, specifically frustration and maybe even a little fear or anger. Such an intense reaction arises from self-doubt about your ability to get the story right.

Indeed, a lot of writing is trial and error. Sometimes what at the outset seems like a middling idea actually turns out to be the best cure. Sometimes what initially appears to be a fantastic idea turns out to be the entirely wrong prescription.

The beauty of writing is that there always are a number of ways to solve any given problem. Suppose the result of your main character's effort to resolve a problem doesn't deliver the necessary gravitas to help your protagonist grow. Simply have your character take an entirely tact toward resolving the issue, specifically one that leads to the result you desire. There are thousands of different approaches your main character might take. Or you might instead tweak the result. Or you might modify how the character grows through the story.

You may need to outline or pen several drafts of a scene to make it work. Whatever you do, keep at it. The satisfaction you feel upon succeeding will be the worth the effort.

>To remove yourself from the story so you can best determine what needs to be changed, set it aside for a few days, then reread. You may find that some of what sounded great when you first penned it is now problematic and that some of what you initially disliked actually reads quite well.

>Have your story critiqued by others – not by a spouse, parents, family members or close friends but by someone who writes, reads or edits for a living (Full disclosure here: I own and run such an editing service.). In addition, have just one or two readers/editors look it over; if you give it to too many people, you'll likely receive conflicting advice that only will make revising more difficult, if not impossible.

>While analyzing your own draft, try deconstructing the piece into the various elements of fiction (plot, setting, character, point of view, theme). This can be beneficial in determining what is missing. Revising the manuscript by focusing on one element at a time probably isn't very workable, however. These elements work together to make an integrated whole, and so the story needs to be approached holistically.

WEEK 46

Like the rising sun, my writing casts an ever-widening light upon the world.

The hours before dawn mark the darkest hours, when seeing even a few feet in front of you is difficult. As night's blanket has covered the world for several hours, the wind blows its coldest and the ground is at its dampest.

And then, at last, a thin line of orange appears on the horizon. The sky about it lightens from an impenetrable black to a friendly blue, and soon tree leaves and sides of buildings shimmer in the glow of the rising sun. Dawn reawakens the world, gives it a fresh start, a new hope.

Your writing – once published – can have the same effect.

As a unique human being, you can offer the world a perspective that was never considered before, can synthesize disparate ideas that offer new insights and solutions, can inspire people to work for great causes and to shift their views away from those that are dark and unjust.

Granted, few books have had such a remarkable impact that they utterly altered human history. But each book published contributes, for better or for worse, to the improvement of humanity. Movements cannot occur, after all, without the push and press of millions of individuals; likewise, shifts in consciousness often occur when thousands of books on an idea are published. Perhaps your book is not as revolutionary as Darwin's "On the Origin of Species" or Harriett Beecher Stowe's "Uncle Tom's Cabin," but it may help direct a new course in thinking that allows for a work of such magnitude to make its impact.

Or perhaps your book will inspire a lone, single reader to take up writing or a cause, and her efforts lead to a titanic change in history. Or perhaps she will pass those ideas on to one of her children, who will have such an effect. History is littered with stories, poems and songs that energized others to improve the world, sometimes generations later. Perhaps such works of art are relegated to footnote status, but their impact reshaped and now drives civilization.

By never publishing, though, you shun an opportunity to make a positive difference. You diminish your potential to change the world.

You allow the world to remain in blackness a little longer.

>*Rather than consume something, when writing we make something. The very act of writing then is a choice in how we'll live and treat our planet. In what other ways does your simple decision to write alter the world around you?*

>*If you could change one thing about the world, what would it be? What could you write that might help facilitate this change?*

>*Why do you write? To feel more fully alive? To give the world meaning and purpose? If your answer is mundane or ego-centric – to make money, to achieve fame – ask if your writing can serve a deeper, more profound aspiration.*

WEEK 47

Your unread story is like a gold nugget buried in a mountain. Dynamite a tunnel for others to discover your treasure.

You've spent a year writing your book, spent money on an editor to proofread it and a designer to create a book cover, then spent a week or two taking it through the self-publishing process. And now, after all of that hard work, your book – your labor of love – is available for purchase with its own page on Amazon.com and can be bought at your local mom and pop bookstore.

All you have to do now is sit back and wait for fame and fortune to roll in.

Unfortunately, you may be waiting a very long time.

It's the rare book that somehow goes viral and captures the public's attention and admiration all on its own. Indeed, your book is buried in the mountain of more than 900 other books that are published daily (in just the United States alone) not to mention all that have been published before and will come in the years ahead. No matter how good yours is, the odds of it even being noticed are nil at best.

The reality is that indie authors and those who self-publish need to promote their own books.

For most authors, the idea of promoting their book is anathema. "Promoting," to many writers, means using guilt and fear to convince people to buy a product. Even for those authors who don't hold such a view, they probably never studied marketing and have no idea of how to begin such an effort.

But unless you're satisfied with your book languishing in anonymity, you need to market it. You'll need to send press releases to media outlets. You'll need a website and probably a blog to inform people about your book. You'll need to do some book signings, some book readings, maybe some radio interviews. You may need to make some business cards and even advertise.

You'll need to dynamite a tunnel through the mountain of published books so that readers can see your gold nugget. Your marketing effort is that tunnel to your book.

Now go on, set the blasting cap and detonator.

>*How do you feel about marketing your book? Why do you hold this view? What are your concerns about spending time promoting your book?*

>*Marketing a book often involves setting up a platform – such as a website, blog, social media sites (including Facebook, LinkedIn and Pinterest) – to let others know about your title. Write a list of the various ways you might reach potential readers of your book.*

>*You'll also want to promote your book by getting in front of people, such as at a book reading or a book signing. Are you comfortable speaking in front of others? If not, what can you do to limit your anxiety ahead of such an event?*

WEEK 48

The energy your writing brings to readers is directly proportional to the amount of energy you bring to your writing.

When writing, *effort* – vigorous and determined work – always counts the most.

Effort is the one thing you can control when writing and publishing a book. Other variables – how many books on the topic are coming out at the same time as your title, those authors' level of expertise and writing abilities, if someone clicks "buy" on your Amazon.com page – are nothing you can really influence. If those variables you can't control do work in your favor, then you've simply enjoyed some good luck.

Effort matters at every stage of the writing process. When brainstorming, it means tossing around a lot of ideas and a willingness to explore ones that are off-the-wall. It means concerted work in creating a detailed outline. When penning the first draft, it means putting in the hard, day-by-day sessions needed to constructing your book word-by-word with all of the necessary research (especially if writing non-fiction). It means penning several drafts of the book until you get it right. And when a final draft is arrived at, it means ensuring the formatting and book cover are professional and that you put in the long but important hours of marketing it.

Of course, no matter how hard you work, uncertainty exists in every writing project. Many questions will remain un-answered: How will readers react to the story? Will a critic trash my book and ruin my sales? Will the cover look good to readers? But if you only hope for the best, you're fatalistic. Effort ensures you'll assess and determine how to best address those areas of uncertainty.

And sure, efficiency and expertise are important. Effort, though, includes learning how not to waste time and how to be ever more competent with your writing skills.

In writing, there are no shortcuts. Put the necessary energy and passion into your work, and your readers will recognize it – and your talent!

>*For novice and unpublished writers, questions often are more important than answers. What are your writing goals? What skills do you need to achieve that goal? How can you learn those skills you don't have?*

>*Exploration is more important than striving, at least initially for a writer learning the craft. Productivity is only relevant in that you keep writing to grow and hone your skills. Once you've reached a certain level of competence, your short story, novel or nonfiction book will be publishable. What are the fundamental skills that a writer should possess? Do you have them? If not, how can you obtain them?*

>*Once you've reached a certain level of competence as a writer, you then must work hard to achieve your goals. For a writer, there's nothing nuanced about hard work. It simply means showing up every day at the computer keyboard and actually writing. How many words or pages do you turn out per day, on average?*

WEEK 49

Never be afraid to write what you believe. If the message speaks the truth, others will fear your words for you.

You're at a cocktail party, are introduced to one of the guests. He asks, "What do you do?"

"I'm a writer," you respond.

"Oh. What do you write?"

At that moment, does your stomach churn with anxiety and your palms go clammy? Do you believe that if telling the truth, you'll be looked down upon, that others behind your back will whisper, "He writes that weird nerdy science fiction stuff...he writes erotica, must be a pervert...she writes trashy hackneyed romances, must not have any talent...she writes that highfalutin literary stuff that no one can understand – and that no one ever buys."

When you're afraid how others will react to your writing, you've allowed them to define you. Should you write only what others find acceptable, you've allowed them to control you. You've given their values a higher priority than your own tastes and standards.

As you writer, you cannot care what others will think of you or your writing. You instead must care about the *truth*.

Of course, "the truth" often is a wide swath of gray. People possess different values, they see the world from unique perspectives, their memories falter over time. But what is *your* truth? What are your values? What is your perspective on the world? What is your memory of an event?

If your strive to be truthful in writing – that is deliberately not contradicting your values, not distorting your perspective, and not altering your memories for personal gain – your words will be authentic. Not all readers may agree with you (and truthfully, you never can please everyone), but they will respect your genuineness.

And perhaps the best response your writing ever can receive is *criticism* of your ethics, viewpoints, and recollections. It means that your writing touched more than a nerve in readers, suggests that others fear what you have to say because *they* have something to lose should the truth be widely known.

So don't mumble your answer and fidget when someone asks what you write. Tell them loudly and confidently what your book is all about. They'll then be the ones whose foreheads break a sweat...or maybe they'll even be the ones who heartily clasp your hands and thank you for what you've written.

>*Being authentic requires that you be in touch with yourself. Ask yourself who you are (That is, how how do you define yourself?). What makes you happy? What are your passions (beyond writing, of course!)? Does your writing reflect who you are and what you feel most strongly about?*

>*Often without realizing it, writers are part of something larger than themselves; that is, they become part of a trend, whether it be in a genre (For example, in the horror genre, vampires were big in the early 2010s but have since given way to zombies.) or in subject matter (such as how-to self-publishing guidebooks during the early 2010s). Is the topic*

matter of your writing part of a trend? If so, what can you do differently so that your writing shapes and influences that trend? What could you write that might start the next trend?

>What is the purpose of your writing? That is, why do you write? What do you hope to accomplish? Now ask if your writing is true to that purpose.

WEEK 50

My words can light the way for someone else on a dark path.

E ven if your book never changes the world – let alone influence other authors in its genre – your writing still can make a difference just by affecting the lives of a few or even of a lone reader.

Suppose you publish a book about how you survived cancer. Your trauma can let readers know they are not going through their fear and radiation treatments alone, that someone else has suffered the same despair, those same "slings and arrows of outrageous fortune." Your triumph can provide the hope and inspiration that they desperately need.

Or perhaps your book gives the reader an idea that becomes their life passion. Maybe the character of your book volunteers, stirring a reader to help at a food pantry and work to end world hunger. Maybe the science fiction story you wrote contains some device that is so cool – portable phones and desktop computers, for example, appeared in many futuristic stories published during the mid-20th century – that a reader works toward inventing it and in doing so changes the world for the better.

You need not write a profound book to make a significant difference in another's life. If penning nonfiction, your book may help others better manage their money, get a date and find love, improve their parenting, discover a new delectable dish to prepare, organize their home, plan their vacation, understand how the world works, and much, much more. In fact, often nonfiction directly affects peoples' lives for the better because it provides valuable information that they're seeking.

Even fiction with no profound message and that serves solely as an escape can help others. Sometimes people need just a few minutes a day to get away from the world's crushing troubles and responsibilities, and your mystery novel or space adventure short story might just be the turn of the valve they need to release some pressure.

Once you publish and get out in public to promote your book, you'll likely meet many readers who will want to share their story of how it affected their lives. You'll be surprised by their stories and the unexpected ways that your words made a difference.

For every reader who had the courage to tell you their story, another dozen never will, as they don't know how to contact you or are too shy. The truth is your book will have a much greater impact than you ever will know.

>*List a half-dozen social issues that you feel passionate about. For the next few days, write journal entries about each one. Do any lead to ideas for stories or books that you might write?*

>*When writing, always keep your readers' needs in mind.*

That doesn't mean you should write solely to please the reader and in doing so be inauthentic. Instead, as you tell your story or make your suggestions, think about what your reader might want to know, and how your wording can help them relate to your book. Readers will appreciate not being talked down to and will recognize that you are not self-consumed.

>If volunteering to ladle food onto plates of the hungry isn't your thing, that doesn't mean you can't make a difference at the soup kitchen. Put your writing skills to work by offering to write press releases, brochures, or other promotional materials for a social cause that you feel strongly about.

WEEK 51

Writing is my way of life.

"You must stay drunk on writing so reality cannot destroy you." — Ray Bradbury

Hopefully, you've spent nearly a year now reading and internalizing the writing affirmations in this book, as well as doing the writing prompts that follow. The entries in this book are based on the premise that several small choices can go a long way toward ensuring large, life-altering changes. Now that a year has almost passed and this book is nearly at its end, the challenge facing you is continuing to write each day, preferably on a book that you've always wanted to publish.

Falling into old habits, though, is easier than maintaining new ones.

To prevent that from occurring, begin each day by reminding yourself who you are: You are a writer, and writing is a way of life for you. Maybe you'll need to scribble that on a piece of paper and tape it to your bathroom mirror so you read it every morning when you brush your teeth (What? You don't brush your teeth every morning? For shame!). After all, if you remind yourself daily to do something, you likely will do it, and soon it becomes habit.

At the end of each day, also remind yourself how much pleasure you derived during your writing session and the good feelings it left you with. Though writing can be hard work, you did receive a reward for it – the satisfaction that comes from being creative, the feeling of accomplishment as your book comes a few hundred words closer to being completed. By focusing on the benefits writing brought you, you'll want to get back at it again tomorrow.

Another way to internalize the writing habit is to hang around people and places who will encourage and reinforce it. For example, join a writers' group or regularly attend book readings. In economics, this is known as "choice architecture," in which the decisions you make are largely based on the choices offered to you. Hence, if you wish to write more, then organize your time so you're around people in which writing, as one of many choices about how you'll spend your free time, looms large.

Simply put, change your habits, and you'll change the outcomes in your life. After all, if you take up gardening, within a few months you'll probably start receiving compliments on your beautiful rose bush. If you want to receive compliments on your book, then take up writing next year (And start brushing your teeth when you wake up, okay?).

>When are you most creative and most productive as a writer? Write a description of that place, noting the time of day,

which of your senses are appealed to during that span, if you use pen and paper or keyboard and computer.

>Give yourself a 30-day challenge. Set aside a time during which you will write for at least a half-hour daily. Can you write during that time period for 30 straight days? If you do, reward yourself...then set another 30-day challenge.

>Goals are landmarks in your life, not definitions of it. If your book requires more time to write than you initially thought, that's okay. Just don't give up on it or be critical of yourself because a goal wasn't made by a certain date on an artificial timeline. Keep working on your writing goals, and when you achieve one of them, celebrate it as the success it is.

WEEK 52

To write is to realize my destiny.

Writing is your destiny.
It's more than just a pattern in your life. It is reaching for your full potential; it is those moments you feel most self-empowered.

When writing, you experience fulfillment and bliss. You feel successful and enjoy affluence, perhaps not yet monetarily but certainly you are showered with the emotional and intellectual wealth that a creative pursuit brings.

When writing, you feel like you are doing exactly what you were placed on this Earth to do. Writing is meaningful, and you have purpose.

It is living your dream.

It is your future.

>Much of this book has focused on encouraging you to believe in yourself as a writer. Look back at the affirmations from the first few weeks. Do you believe they are true, that they apply to you?

>What is the legacy you wish to leave? Each of us has a limited time on Earth. How in that short time – through your writing – might you make the world a better place for future generations?

>What is your big, seemingly impossible, goal as writer? To write a nonfiction book? To publish a short story? List the steps you must take to achieve this vision. Now work on achieving each one of those smaller steps as you head toward your big goal.

About the Author

Rob Bignell is the owner and chief editor of Inventing Reality Editing Service, which meets the editing and proofreading needs of writers both new and published. Several of his short stories in the literary and science fiction genres have been published, and he is the author of the literary novel "Windmill," the nonfiction "7 Minutes a Day...," "Best Sights to See," "Hikes with Tykes," "Headin' to the Cabin," and "Hittin' the Trail" guide-books, and the poetry collection "Love Letters to Sophie's Mom." For more than two decades, he worked as an award-winning journalist, with half of those years spent as an editor. He spent another seven years as an English teacher or a community college journalism instructor. He holds a Master's degree in English and a Bachelor's in journalism and English.

CHECK OUT THESE TITLES IN THE '7 MINUTES A DAY...' WRITING GUIDEBOOKS

➤ **7 Minutes a Day to Your Bestseller** – Novel writers receive expert advice on topics like motivating yourself to write, starting your story with exciting opening lines, creating intriguing characters, mastering the craft of writing to elevate your style, and pitching your story to potential publishers.

➤ **7 Minutes a Day to a Self-Published Book** – Whether writing a novel or nonfiction, whether planning to print a paperback or an ebook, this book guides you through the self-publishing process, from the title page to the index, from designing a cover to formatting your text.

➤ **7 Minutes a Day to Promoting Your Book** – You'll develop a strategy that will get articles about your self-published book in newspapers, magazines, on radio and television programs, posted on blogs, and linked to on websites, while landing you book signings and readings, all at virtually no cost.

➤ **7 Minutes a Day to Mastering the Craft of Writing** – Craft is as important to storytelling as the plot or characters. This book gives you 50 tried-and-true techniques to improve your writing craftsmanship, including using active voice, showing not telling, ramping up dramatic tension, and being more descriptive.

ORDER ONLINE
inventingrealityediting.
wordpress.com/home/my-books

WANT TO BECOME A BETTER WRITER?

Follow this book's blog,
where you'll find:

☞Advice for making your
writing stronger

☞Great tips
about self-publishing

☞Questions about writing
and marketing answered

☞Product reviews

☞News about the book series
and author

VISIT ONLINE
inventingrealityeditingservice.typepad.
com/inventing_reality_editing/

NEED
AN EDITOR?

Having your book, business document or academic paper proofread or edited before submitting it can prove invaluable. In an economic climate where you face heavy competition, your writing needs a second eye to give you the edge. The author of this title and the "7 Minutes a Day..." writing guidebook series can provide that second eye.

FIND OUT MORE AT:
inventingrealityediting.
wordpress.com/home

Made in the USA
San Bernardino, CA
03 August 2019